THE COMPLETE G

Homeschooling

THE COMPLETE GUIDE TO

Homeschooling

John and Kathy Perry

LOWELL HOUSE

LOS ANGELES

NTC/Contemporary Publishing Group

Library of Congress Cataloging-in-Publication Data

Perry, John, 1959–

 The complete guide to homeschooling / by John and Kathy Perry.

  p. cm.

 Includes bibliographical references (p. 241) and index.

 ISBN 0-7373-0422-7 (pbk.)

  1. Homeschooling—United States. I. Perry, Kathy, 1959– II. Title.

 LC40.P47 2000

 371.04'2—dc21   00-057931

Published by Lowell House

A division of NTC/Contemporary Publishing Group, Inc.

4255 West Touhy Avenue, Lincolnwood, Illinois 60712, U.S.A.

Managing Director and Publisher: Jack Artenstein

Executive Editor: Peter L. Hoffman

Director of Publishing Services: Rena Copperman

Editor: Claudia McCowan

Managing Editor: Jama Carter

Project Editor: Carmela Carvajal

Design by Kate Mueller

Printed in the United States of America

International Standard Book Number: 0-7373-0422-7

00 01 02 03 04 DHD 18 17 16 15 14 13 12 11 10 9 8 7 6 5 4 3 2 1

ACKNOWLEDGMENTS

Steven & Jeff, our sons,

You still love us despite having to read Mom's favorite book, *Jane Eyre*. We miss the hours spent homeschooling together. You were our teachers.

Albert Misciskia, Sonny Papa,

When we first told you we wrote a book, you asked if it was a Western. That's just one more thing we owe you. You've loved us, supported us, and been proud of all we've done. We are who we are because of you.

James Perry, Great Poppy,

What can we say about a ninety-two-year-old great-grandfather, other than "You're the greatest!"

Hudson Perigo, our editor,

Sometimes when publishing a book, the author only meets the editor by phone. Hudson's voice radiates an enchanting tone, one that a baby would find a lullaby. Hudson, without your patience, guidance, and friendship, this book would never have been published.

We also wish to thank Executive Editor Peter Hoffman, Project Editor Carmela Carvajal, and the rest of the dedicated people at Lowell House Publishing.

CONTENTS

Effectively • Homework or No Homework, That Is the Question! • The Importance of Meeting a Deadline • Keeping Good Records • Homeschooling More Than One Child at a Time • Homeschoolers Learn to Use Their Time Wisely • Motivating a Child • Homeschooling 8:00 to 3:00 • How Many Hours Per Day Should We Homeschool? • Year-Round Schooling • Are You a Morning Person? • Beginning the Process • An Ideal Teacher • How Does My Child Learn? • Helpful Hints for Starting • Repeat Courses as Review • Teaching a Course Too Quickly • In Summary

Kindergarten Through Fifth Grade • Beginning in the Elementary Years • Evaluate Your Child's Situation • What to Teach • Homeschooling Styles • It's Fun to Homeschool • Hyperactivity or Attention Deficit Disorder • The Physically Challenged Child • Museums, Art Galleries, the Zoo • Report Cards • The School Bus, the Lunch Line, the PTO • Holidays and Vacation Days • Immunizations • Reading for the Elementary Student • Manipulatives • Reentering Public or Private School • In Summary

Preteen Years, Emotional Years • Where Did They Go Wrong? • Caution: Teenager in the Room • The Emotional Middle School Child • The Middle Schooler's Social Life • Report Cards • Learning Is Retaining • Grading Fairly • Yearly Testing Requirements • Homework for the Middle Schooler • Specific Middle School Course Suggestions • High School Credits • Da Vinci, Renoir, Picasso, and Rauschenberg • Artistic Expression • Drop Down and Give Me Twenty • Expelled from the Public School • Homeschooling Just for a Year or Two • A Note Regarding High School Credits • In Summary

So You Have a High School Homeschooler! • Last Chance to Work on the Fundamentals • These Are the Scary Years—Help! • Courses Available • Don't Forget the Fine Arts • High

FOREWORD

John and Kathy Perry have formulated the most comprehensive work I have ever read on homeschooling. I have treated thousands of children and adolescents, and many of their parents have been interested in homeschooling. *The Complete Guide to Homeschooling* is my number-one reference guide for these families.

Parents ask: Why would I want to homeschool? Is it legal to homeschool in my state? Do I need a special degree or certificate to teach my children at home? Will my children still have access to school sports? How do I get started? What materials are available to me to teach my children? How do I test my children to see if they are learning? Will colleges look at my homeschooled children the same as other children? Are there computer software programs that can help with homeschooling? Can we afford homeschooling? *The Complete Guide to Homeschooling* will answer these questions and more.

Homeschooling has become a valuable alternative to today's public school process. Yes, there are some great public schools and incredibly gifted teachers, but for every successful school system there are ten that are not successful, where children are not educated appropriately, and values are completely lost. As John and Kathy Perry point out, education in America is failing in many school systems. Children often are not taught how to think and solve problems, how to use available resources, or how to interact with adults.

In response to the question "I worry that my children will lack the social skills that everyone professes they acquire by attending public schools," John and Kathy Perry respond: "Our children were the first to notice that homeschooling gave them confidence in their self-worth. They admitted that they felt intelligent enough to convey their opinions when talking to adults. We taught them to ask questions and gave them the will to want to learn more. . . . We address social concerns throughout this book because they are a big factor to consider when choosing to homeschool your child."

How do homeschooled children respond when they reenter the public school system? The authors write: "One of the things [their youngest son] expressed was that he wasn't afraid to talk with his teachers, ask questions, or give his opinion. Most of his teachers were surprised at how well he related to them with confidence. We received compliments on his attitude."

Ralph Waldo Emerson said, "Character is higher than intellect." We have removed the process of teaching values in our schools, which I believe has been the worst educational decision ever made. Values and having a value structure is the most important piece of education for all of our children. We are teaching information and not values or character building in our schools. You may ask, "Whose values should be taught?" True values belong to no particular group, no particular religion, no particular country, but are basic truths and standards of living we must strive toward to live in a harmonious society. Values such as honesty, integrity, courage, passion, compassion, empathy, discipline, love, forgiveness, persistence, and humor are all immensely important in the upbringing and education of a child anywhere on Earth. They belong to no one yet must be a part of everyone for our society to survive and thrive in a harmonious and compassionate way.

Parents are the first educators of their children, and as I discuss in my book, *Brilliant Babies, Powerful Adults: Awaken the Genius Within*, the process starts during pregnancy. *The Complete Guide to Homeschooling* will answer your questions and guide you on the path of homeschooling. This is by far the best tool for homeschooling in the market today.

John M. Mike, M.D.
http://www.smart-baby.com

INTRODUCTION

Welcome to Homeschooling Without Fear

Like us, you are disappointed in the public school system today. You've probably experienced frustration, unsuccessful parent/teacher conferences, poor-quality curricula, crowded classrooms, and safety concerns. You may feel that you've exhausted all possibilities for improvement and are at a loss about what to do. The answer is extremely simple: *Homeschool your child!*

You say, "Easier said than done. I wouldn't know where or how to begin." The thought of having to educate your own child is a bit frightening, and you wonder if you are qualified to do the job. Your questions are mounting, and you would love to ask a successful homeschooling parent for the answers.

We are those parents, and we'll prove how easily homeschooling can be accomplished. Whether you plan to homeschool from the elementary through high school years, or simply for a year or two to strengthen your child's academic skills, this book will give you a place to start. Consider us your guides to the homeschooling experience.

> Consider us your guides to the homeschooling experience.

Ironically, we looked for a book like this when we first decided to try homeschooling. We needed an easy, straightforward question-and-answer forum on homeschooling information.

Searching the Web for answers wasn't as easy as we had been told, for many of the Web sites didn't supply direct-access information. We knew nothing about the homeschooling community or how to get in touch with other homeschooling families. Several of the books we purchased (we bought just about every one pertaining to homeschooling) gave us an abundance of reasons why we should homeschool, but not enough information on how to begin. Besides, most parents know why they want to homeschool; they're just fearful of the process. So, armed with our own homeschooling experience and that of several homeschooling friends and families we've met along the way, we're happy to provide you with the "how-tos" of homeschooling.

Our Story: The Decision to Homeschool

The decision to teach our children at home was reached quite easily. The public school system made it for us. Our oldest son was attending middle school in a top-rated school district just outside of Houston, Texas. Most middle schools consist of normal sixth graders, monster seventh graders, and hormonal eighth graders. Our son was no exception. He was first chair in the honors band, participated in many school activities, and maintained a fair grade point average. He had goals, an excellent attitude toward school, and good friends. He was a unique individual who soon became a statistic.

This unique individual, a grown man today, defended an innocent bystander from a bully and paid dearly for the effort, for the bully was a known gang leader with a string of friends who targeted our son as his next victim. And victim he was, of beatings, verbal abuse, and threats to himself and his younger brother, who was attending elementary school. The old school of thought on how to take care of a bully had been replaced with the fear that the bully now carried a weapon.

The school realized the situation and provided for the safety of both our sons by giving them interdistrict transfers. So, you see, it changed our oldest son's life, his younger brother's life, and our lives, overnight. This bright student said goodbye to friends, teachers, sports, clubs, and life as he knew it, all with the bravest outlook for his future not many twelve-year-old boys possess. We're not so sure we could have been as brave as he had been, walking down the hall corridor after saying goodbye to a teary-eyed

> **We didn't automatically decide to homeschool, because we didn't think we were the homeschooling type.**

band director, who shook her head in disbelief and whispered, "How unjust the system is."

Desperate Measures

We think of ourselves as capable and strong parents able to provide the best for our children. However, we felt powerless, something parents dread having to experience while raising their children. The thing was, we didn't automatically decide to homeschool, because we didn't think we were the homeschooling type. We weren't even sure what that type of person truly was.

We began interviewing the private schools. We thought that paying for an education would solve everything. Our son would continue with his goals in a private school environment that probably housed better teachers, curricula, and safety measures. But we noticed something about the many private schools we visited. We felt we would be paying for economic and cultural segregation, and that wasn't a message we wanted our children to learn.

We were desperate; we had two sons uprooted from their structured education looking to us for guidance. Face it, weren't we supposed to make sure our children were educated in the best schools by the best teachers? Wasn't the whole idea to max out on the biggest house we could afford, placing our children in a wealthy school district? Wealthy school districts have better teachers, right? We all can vouch for that inaccuracy. Working longer hours to live in wealthier neighborhoods does not produce better-educated children.

Was Homeschooling Something We Resorted To?

As a very last resort, and we're extremely embarrassed to admit that fact now, we discussed homeschooling. But wasn't homeschooling something that the Amish people did? And how exactly did *they* do it?

Considering homeschooling as an option for our children was the real question. We wish this book had been available when we began the process of homeschooling, for we learned by trial and error.

How to Use This Book

Scattered throughout this book are stories from homeschoolers who have graduated, are in college or the workforce, or are even married and homeschooling their own children. We had a wonderful time conducting the research to find these graduates, and only wish we could have included all the responses we received. You'll find open and honest quotes from each graduate, and we hope you enjoy them as much as we did.

Additionally, we have to apologize to each graduate by saying that a few paragraphs do great injustice to their wonderful homeschooling experiences, but that we are privileged to be able to include them in our book.

We've prepared answers to the most frequently asked questions parents consider when deciding to homeschool. We supply you with the pros and cons, the ups and downs, and the joys and woes of homeschooling. Ultimately, you'll make the choice of whether homeschooling fits your lifestyle. We recommend that you read the questions in the order they're presented to receive a clear overall understanding of homeschooling. Consider this your conversation with experienced and successful homeschoolers who want to answer your questions. Additionally, we'll refer to organizations, books, periodicals, and Web sites that will interest you. So, let us introduce ourselves. We are John and Kathy Perry, confident and successful homeschooling parents, and we're very pleased to answer your homeschooling questions.

CHAPTER 1

Beginning the Challenge

What You Need to Know Before Beginning

Before we answer any questions, you need to know that you are not the first parent to consider homeschooling. Homeschoolers are almost 1.7 million strong. We are no longer hiding the fact that we educate our children. Homeschooling is a socially acceptable means of education in today's American society.

Although it may seem frightening picturing yourself as a homeschooler, realize we felt the same way when we began. Before we dive into answering your homeschooling questions, we want to share how each of us approached homeschooling.

Kathy's Story

It was the evening before our first day of homeschooling. The plan was in place and ready to be set into motion. John and I had decided to plunge into homeschooling, but I have to admit I'm not the type to dive into a pool headfirst. In fact, I'm afraid of water. I test the water temperature, one toe at a time, and if it's too cold I think twice before jumping in at all. All the homeschooling research was about to be put to the test. I had the books, the supplies, and the right outlook. Something was missing.

It was late, and I should have been in bed. Instead, I was wandering around the house finding things to clean. Maybe that was what was wrong, because I only clean when I'm scared, confused, or angry. So, my house is usually a mess.

The house felt extremely silent as I thumbed through the new textbooks poised on the kitchen table, a table that over the next several years would earn its place in our home. I told myself it was time to get a good night's rest. My inner voice screamed, "Go to bed."

> I so needed to hear that we were doing the right thing by deciding to homeschool our children.

I climbed into bed, wondering how my husband could sleep on the eve of such an important undertaking. I found myself softly crying tears of anxiety. I so needed to hear that we were doing the right thing by homeschooling our children. More important, as the children's primary teacher, I needed someone to tell me I was qualified to take on such a task. I was their mom; I would become their teacher. Would I live up to my own expectations?

My husband held me close and whispered, "Everything is going to be fine. You are a wonderful mother; now you will be a wonderful teacher. We will get through this, you'll see. More than half the battle is won. You already have their love and respect. They are ready to learn."

I awoke early from a good night's rest, ready to embark on my new career. The boys were sitting at the kitchen table eager to begin, and I returned their smiles. Not so many years ago, I had brought them home from the hospital and promised myself I'd be a good mother. Who would have thought I'd become their teacher? For the first time in my life I realized that I was the best person to understand their educational needs. I knew when they were ill, or tired, or frustrated. Now I would be expected to know whether they could read, understand, and retain their schoolwork.

I dove headfirst that day into the water, and I kept on swimming until they could swim without me. It was an effort. It was a commitment. It was hard work. Without a doubt, I'd do it all over again, for I became the student, and they became my teachers. I gave them the gift of an excellent education. They gave me the gift of confidence.

John's Story

My wife and I, after briefly researching homeschooling, decided to give it a try for one year. I admit it changed her life more than my own. I still got up and went to work as usual, knowing my family members were busy at home with their studies. I would call at lunch and check on their day, sometimes being asked to help solve a mathematical problem or listen to a tidbit they had just discovered.

Life for our family changed in many ways. I noticed my sons were less stressed about getting their schoolwork finished on time and more excited about the learning process. In the evening they talked endlessly about books they had read, problems they had solved, and experiments they had conducted. They loved the freedom of going outside for science, helping each other with their courses, and teaching Mom the things she pretended not to grasp as quickly as they did.

For Christmas, our children asked for a telescope instead of video games. They shut the television off in the evening to debate who had the correct answers on independent work. And I observed my wife's tears of accomplishment. My wife and I exchanged many a proud smile, knowing we'd done the right thing.

I often apologized to my wife for not being able to be the primary teacher. I saw how tired she was in the evening preparing for the next day. Nevertheless, she selflessly said, "I could never have homeschooled our children without you holding down the full-time job. That was every bit of teaching your sons priorities and supportiveness in a family." We may have had reservations about beginning the homeschooling process, but we certainly had outstanding success throughout the endeavor.

> **For Christmas, our children asked for a telescope instead of video games.**

Steven's Story

Not only did my schooling change when I was just twelve, but my perspective on life changed, too. Over the years, I've been asked if I was ever bitter, having had to homeschool. The answer has always been "Never." Yes, as a young boy I wanted revenge on the bully I encountered, but today, as an adult, I would thank him.

I had always been a good student in school. Yes, I struggled with some courses like other kids, waited until the last minute to study or turn in a project, and sweet-talked my mom into reading my assigned books. I was more involved in athletics and band, and the only reason I maintained a decent grade point average was so I could play ball and travel with the honors band. I was the typical guy in school. I checked out the girls, joined the popular activities and clubs, and strutted my stuff. I was headed for the life of the school jock and all-around popular guy.

Now, ask me if I could read well. Back then, I would have bragged that I was doing just fine, but the fact is, I only got by. Any of the difficult assignments I had were pawned off on my mom or a girlfriend. I sweet-talked teachers and volunteered to help rearrange desks, bookcases, and anything else that would help with my grade. I respected the teachers, and in turn, they liked me. Ah, life was cool.

> My parents approached homeschooling with me as a "let's take it one year at a time" process.

You've read our story, so you know everything changed for me. The only regret I ever had was the impact this had on the life of my younger brother, Jeff. He was in elementary school when all this happened, and what affected me doubly affected him.

My parents had justified homeschooling as a "let's take it one year at a time" process. Probably, if they had said they were giving up on the public school system and announced we would become avid homeschoolers, I would have objected. But knowing I tested at three grade levels below where I should have been bothered me. They offered to help set me back on track academically, and I offered to give it a shot for one year.

Well, the rest is history, and obviously I homeschooled longer than a year. I received an excellent education because I gave it my all. And, yes, I wish the homeschooling sports program had had more to offer, but I didn't suffer because of it. I entered college at sixteen, doubled in a vocational program for automobile technology as well, and carried a part-time job through it all. I learned the value of an education through hard work and dedication. Best of all, I realized the value of a family that cares.

So, to my little brother, I'm proud of how we taught each other, but I still can run rings around you in literature. Yes, I'm an auto mechanic who can quote Shakespeare. We're not all grease monkeys. To my parents, you know I appreciate all that you have done and continue to do. And, to myself, well . . . "You did a good job of giving it a try for a year."

Jeffrey's Story

I'm the younger, better-looking brother. At first, when my mom and dad asked me to write my story, I was a bit reluctant, for I have a different perspective on homeschooling than my brother, Steve.

In the beginning, when my brother faced some difficult times, I have to admit I was a little scared for him and for me. I knew for a fact that I didn't want to enter his middle school if I had to worry about my safety. At the time, I was in the fifth grade, and the thought of having to change schools, go to a private school, or homeschool seemed unreal. None was what I wanted to do. It felt as if I didn't have any "say-so" in the situation, and when I think back on that time, my parents agreed they didn't give me a choice.

> Well, I hate to admit my parents were right, but they were.

So, homeschooling began and actually wasn't too bad. I had the freedom to get up and get something to drink while we did our lessons. When I needed to stretch, Mom left it up to me to take a break. Anxiety and the pressure of having to complete work in a hurried fashion simply didn't exist. I have to admit that part was great.

Still, something always seemed to be missing. My parents assumed it was the extracurricular activities, so they made sure I joined all the available homeschooling sports and activities. I enjoyed everything we did, from spelling bees to state basketball tournaments. I had homeschooling friends, public schooled friends, and neighborhood friends, but still, I wasn't quite happy.

I excelled quickly, sometimes listening to my mom and brother working on his high school courses. When they weren't looking, I solved his algebra and geometry problems. When he got the answer wrong, I corrected him. I enjoyed that part. I really liked the science and history supplements that my parents prepared. I could have lived without all the literature and poetry, though.

When Steven went off to college the house got quiet, and I have to admit my incentive for working hard started to decline—not that I missed him or anything! My parents decided that I didn't feel challenged, and confessed that at the rate I'd been learning, it looked as if I'd graduate at the age of fourteen. So, the decision was made to send me back to public school. I was appalled; here they went again and made the decision for me. Public high school?

They explained their reasoning and told me I wasn't to worry about my academics, but rather to focus on making new friends and joining as many extracurricular activities as I wanted. They knew how much I loved golf, so they threw in a few things like "Join the golf team," and "We'll get you new clubs."

Well, I hate to admit my parents were right, but they were. Thanks to homeschooling, I don't have to worry about my grades. I've made lots of new friends, some of whom are previous homeschoolers like me. Homeschoolers seem to find each other no matter where we are. I thrive on the classroom competition, and I have to admit sometimes I challenge the teachers—respectfully, of course. I still think of myself as a homeschooler at heart, and I know I always will. Oh, and by the way, I did make the varsity golf team.

Meeting All of Us

Well, you've heard from everyone in our family other than Ariel and Wyatt, our beautiful collies. If they could talk, and we swear sometimes they can, they'd give you their opinions on homeschooling, too. They would plop themselves at our feet when our school day began, and then move to the family room with us when we read. They've heard every classic we've read, especially enjoying *Where the Red Fern Grows.* We've given them "Attentive" awards each year.

We wish to dedicate this book to Ariel, a true homeschooler at heart, for she is at the end of her time with our family. Ariel, we thank you for all the years of protecting us from the mail carrier, the UPS delivery person, and the utility meter readers who invaded our homeschool while we learned. You truly earned your high school diploma.

Terms to Know

The following terms are being used by the media and the homeschooling community, and throughout this book.

Homeschooling: Also home schooling, home-schooling, home education, parent/child education, home-tutoring, and many other variations. Defined as education received in the home, usually taught by the parent.

Umbrella programs: Also referred to as correspondence or satellite schools. An umbrella program is defined as an institution or private school that assists the homeschooling parent with curriculum, testing, and documentation for a fee.

ISPs: Independent Study Programs are curriculum programs obtained from umbrella or correspondence schools.

Teacher: That's you!

Student: That's your child and you!

The classroom: The world is your oyster. Your classroom has no boundaries.

Curriculum: Anything and everything that you will use to educate your child, not limited to textbooks.

Supplements: Anything and everything that you choose to teach your child, above and beyond what your state-mandated courses are.

Required subjects: Those subjects mandated by your state and
   local authorities.

Each question will lead you on a journey toward learning
about homeschooling your child. All you have to do is put forth
some time to read each question and its answer. Let's begin with
the most-asked question: Is it legal to homeschool?

Aren't all the laws against you teaching your own child?

Won't a truant officer come to your door and arrest you?

Is it considered a valid and legal education?

Can you be arrested for doing that?

Do you have to file some type of legal form to homeschool?

Is it legal to homeschool?

A definite yes in all fifty states and Washington, D.C. This is
why you are seeing a homeschooler on every block. So, let's make
it known for those considering this option that it is definitely legal
in the United States.

The Homeschool Legal Defense Association (HSLDA) will provide you with the specific legalities of your own state. Some states
require teaching qualifications, impose regulations on those permitted to conduct the homeschooling, demand registration or reporting to specific state officials, and require testing or mandatory
evaluation. Learn these rules, post them on your refrigerator, and
be thankful you live in the United States of America, where you
are given the opportunity to choose homeschooling as an educational option. Which brings us to the next question.

Are some states easier to homeschool in than others?

This, too, is a definite yes. Some states impose no restrictions
on homeschooling families, making the entire schooling process
relatively simple. Others make the process a little more compli-
cated, but not impossible. State Web sites and organizations are
listed in chapter 10. Contact your state organization for the legal
specifics.

How do I join the Homeschool Legal Defense Association?

Call or write to request an application and a free copy of your state's homeschooling laws. The annual fee for joining HSLDA is $100 per family, discounted when you join a homeschooling support group.

HSLDA
P.O. Box 159
Paeonia Springs, VA 20219
(540) 338-5600
http://www.hslda.org

Is it mandatory to join HSLDA?

No, not at all. But, we were proud to become members of HSLDA, even if it was just for the peace of mind of having someone who knew the homeschooling laws and was prepared to defend our right to educate our children. HSLDA personally assists members in their defense by covering all lawyer fees, expert witness fees, court costs, and expenses allowed by state law.

I've heard that some homeschoolers purchase legal insurance. Is this necessary?

No. Legal insurance isn't necessary because families are almost never taken to court just because they homeschool. Most of the time, court cases deal with much larger disputes. Beware of organizations that recommend legal insurance for the homeschooling family.

Should I contact my own attorney and inform him of my decision to homeschool if I decide not to join HSLDA?

There is no need to keep an attorney on retainer just because you are going to homeschool. If you wish to talk with your attorney about the legalities of homeschooling in your state, to get accurate information, that is up to you. You don't have anything to worry about if you are truly educating your child. Homeschooling means "school at home."

Parents' Rights is a quarterly newsletter from an active homeschooling group in St. Louis, Missouri. This group participates in legal action and hosts educational conferences, in addition to many other activities. The yearly subscription is $15, including postage. Contact it at:

Parents' Rights
12571 Northwinds Dr.
St. Louis, MO 63146
(314) 434-4171

What do I need to know before I withdraw my child from her current school system?

This is where it is essential that you know your state's laws on homeschooling, for some states require that you have a curriculum in place before withdrawing your child. Usually withdrawing your child from school is a simple process, but sometimes you run into an official having a bad day. You want to have the upper hand when talking to school officials. This is possible by knowing your state's homeschooling guidelines. Visit http://www.hslda.org for a listing of each state's individual homeschooling laws and guidelines.

A National Homeschooling Organization

Is there a national organization that provides all the rules and regulations associated with homeschooling that I must join?

We know homeschoolers who were informed by their area school districts that before withdrawing their children from the public school system, they needed to join a national homeschooling organization. There are state homeschooling laws, but there isn't a national organization that you must join. Again, beware of school officials who tell you there is a national organization you must join. That is a false statement.

Is there a form I must file before homeschooling my child?

This will depend on your state's regulations. Some states may require you to state the curriculum you've selected. Some may ask for the name of the individual doing the actual home-schooling. Others may request that your name be placed on a mailing list for mandatory testing. Once you've contacted your state organization, you'll have the answer.

Beware of school districts that re-quire families to file reports of their in-tentions to homeschool. This is not a mandatory requirement in every state. Learn your state's homeschooling laws.

> It is the freedom of teaching our children in the way we see fit that is treasured by homeschooling parents.

Shouldn't there be a national organization that provides regulations for the prospective homeschooler to follow?

We thought it would be a good idea if there were a national organization to regulate homeschooling families, too, until we began homeschooling. This question is the one that makes the majority of the people we meet, who are curious about home-schooling, so angry. People seem to think there should be some organization that regulates or monitors the way children are taught at home. We understand their concern. It is based on the fact that they know dropouts who profess to be homeschoolers. We know them, too, and as you read this book you will discover that dropouts are not considered homeschoolers.

Maybe someday there will be national regulations for home-schooling, though we will probably be on the Capitol steps protesting if that day arrives. For now, homeschoolers would rather have fewer rules to follow. Isn't that, after all, one of the reasons we do not want our children in public schools? It is the freedom of teaching our children in the way we see fit that is treasured by homeschooling parents.

Does a state organization provide the information I'll need to get started homeschooling?

Some information will be provided, but certainly not everything you will need. Most state organizations will send you a packet of information listing pertinent facts. The day our state information arrived was the day homeschooling became a reality instead of speculation.

If I contact my state homeschooling organization, will I automatically have to homeschool my child?

No. You will be requesting information. Your name will not appear on some legal form that notifies your child's school district of your intentions or curiosity about homeschooling. Homeschooling information is provided to the public, not just those who choose to homeschool.

I've heard that some cities are imposing daytime curfews on students. How does that affect the homeschooler?

With the crime rate escalating among teenagers today, trying to promote a safe community is understandable. Therefore, daytime curfews are being imposed in many cities for the sake of safety and to prevent truancy. The tough part arises when the homeschooler needs to be out without a parent during what are considered regular school hours—to work at a part-time job, for example. Homeschoolers don't need an entire day for their school studies and often participate in volunteer activities or have part-time jobs. Curfew laws make this difficult for the homeschooling teen.

Homeschooling families are working to fight these curfew laws and protect the civil rights of our children. You need to read as much information as you can about this situation and its effect

LAND HEINTZBERGER

"The greatest benefit of homeschooling for me was the freedom I had to pursue my own academic interests at my own pace," says Land Heintzberger. *"From homeschooling I learned the self-motivation and self-discipline that have served me so well in sports. Because of the time I devoted to sports, I needed to adjust my school schedule around my training."* He adds, *"The negative impact that this freedom had was that, at times, I didn't spend as much time on subjects that I didn't enjoy as much and was weaker in. I was able to find a solution to that problem by working with tutors."*

Land, a homeschool graduate, is preparing for his lifelong goal of competing in the modern pentathlon at the 2004 Olympics. Land and his sister homeschooled for social and philosophic reasons, and because of the greater freedom it allowed them in their studies. This talented young man was twice USPC Tetrathlon National Champion and represented the United States at tetrathlon competitions in Canada, Ireland, England, and Scotland.

Land entered college early, was on the dean's list, and was named to *Who's Who Among Students in American Junior Colleges*. He graduated from Isothermal Community College with honors, receiving an associate of arts degree. He then went on to graduate from Wofford College with a bachelor of arts in history. At Wofford he lettered twice in cross-country and once in outdoor track, and was the president of the fencing club. He has competed at the Modern Pentathlon Junior World Championships in Prague, Czech Republic; the Junior Pan-American Championships in Hunt, Texas, receiving the team silver and individual bronze medals; the U.S. Open World Cup in San Antonio, Texas; and the U.S. Junior National Championships, where he won the silver medal.

on homeschoolers in your area. It may be a regulation your home-schooler will be facing.

Do some states require standardized testing?

Yes. At the time of this writing some states require standardized testing or evaluation. If you live in a state that requires standardized testing, your state organization will give you the needed information.

Those states that require standardized testing or evaluation don't necessarily enforce testing directly; it can be done by the state or local education agency, state board, or state school chief. Sometimes testing or evaluation can be performed by a certified teacher, with the parents allowed to choose from a list of standardized tests.

Require Standardized Testing

Alaska	Iowa	New Mexico	South Carolina
Arkansas	Louisiana	New York	South Dakota
Colorado	Maine	North Carolina	Tennessee
Connecticut	Massachusetts	North Dakota	Vermont
Delaware	Minnesota	Ohio	Virginia
Florida	Nebraska	Oregon	Washington
Georgia	Nevada	Pennsylvania	West Virginia
Hawaii	New Hampshire	Rhode Island	

Don't Require Standardized Testing

Alabama	Indiana	Mississippi	Texas
Arizona	Kansas	Missouri	Utah
California	Kentucky	Montana	Wisconsin
Idaho	Maryland	New Jersey	Wyoming
Illinois	Michigan	Oklahoma	

What is a homeschool support group?

We're so glad you asked. Well, we have suggested you join a homeschool support group, but right now you are wondering if the people who join those groups sit in a circle and discuss personal problems related to homeschooling, just like those addiction support groups. You're thinking you don't need to sit and bare your soul, cry, or complain about the current public school system. Relax; the support groups aren't quite like that.

Not all of them sit in circles (the circles are getting much too large). They meet in libraries, churches, homes, or even the park. These organized homeschooling parents keep you up-to-date with state and federal legislative homeschooling information. As a matter of fact, an attorney friend volunteered to keep up on the state legalities involving homeschooling for our support group. He was a valuable asset to our support group.

Support groups provide answers to your questions and invite speakers to enlighten the group about particular topics of interest to a homeschooler. They keep you motivated in your quest for a better education for your child. Members share stories about their homeschooling techniques, trade and sell their used curricula, and become audiences for your child to give speeches and oral book reports. They organize group field trips, and have picnics and covered-dish suppers. And they are always willing to lend an ear. Support groups will keep you abreast of the homeschooling events in your area such as book fairs and conventions. HSLDA offers discounted joining fees to members of homeschooling support groups.

Do I need to join other organizations?

No, but you might want to join a homeschool support group to meet families who are pursuing the same educational goals as you. Getting started can be a lonely process. Support groups are composed of experienced homeschooling families.

If you can't locate a homeschooling support group in your area, start one.

We are surprised at the many families homeschooling in seclusion, not because of fear, but because they haven't actively pursued other homeschooling families. We interviewed homeschooling families and asked why they chose not to join support groups. Many felt the support groups were centered on a religious view of homeschooling, rather than an academic one. There are many types of support groups. Visit one, visit several, but try to find one that fits your needs. Your child will benefit greatly from the social interaction.

Where would I find a homeschooling support group in my area? Do homeschooling support groups advertise in the Yellow Pages?

Check the bulletin boards at the library, churches, and youth centers. You may be sitting next to someone in church who is a homeschooler; ask him if he belongs to a support group. Someday, we hope to see homeschooling support groups listed in the Yellow Pages.

If you can't locate a support group near your home, start one.

CLARE HUGHES

"Life is the curriculum, and the world is the classroom. We occasionally used books from the public school, Miquon Math Labs, Key Curriculum math workbooks, English grammar workbooks, Reader's Digest, *and Na-*tional Geographic. *However, everything else was through reading, lots and lots and lots of reading. We simply viewed every minute of every day as a learning opportunity. We went everywhere with our parents and participated in every community activity that they did. Though we lived in the country, we were always quite involved in our community."*

Clare Hughes has been studying ballet since she was seven and is a ballerina and assistant teacher with the Mid-Ohio Valley Ballet Company in West Virginia. The company tours and presents performances for Arts in Education. Clare's repertoire includes roles in *The Nutcracker, A Midsummer Night's Dream, The Tempest, Romeo and Juliet, The Dancing Princesses, The Gift of the Magi, The Legend of Sleepy Hollow, Rumpelstiltskin,* and currently *A Little*

If you would like to do this, the state organizations will provide you with ideas and copies of bylaws from other organizations. Community newspapers and radio stations will provide free public service announcements to promote your meetings and activities. Prepare yourself for a multitude of children at any homeschooling event.

Homeschooling vs. Private School

What benefits are there to homeschooling that I couldn't get by enrolling my child in a private school?

We made a comparison list based on the private schools we interviewed. There are superb private schools in the United States, just as there are excellent teachers in the public schools. There's

---

Princess. She says, "I dance because I love it, and I want to share my talent with other people."

Clare explains that the decision to homeschool was made by her parents even before she was born, though as Clare and her brother got older, they were given the choice to attend a public school or homeschool. Both chose to continue homeschooling.

Perhaps one of the reasons Clare's family was extremely successful in awakening the "need" for knowledge in their children is that they chose not to have a television. The area where they lived had terrible reception, and they simply didn't see the point in spending money on a satellite dish. We could all stand to turn the television off more often.

Clare tells prospective homeschoolers, "You will not be denying your children a social life just because you choose to homeschool. I acquired more social skills working at a grocery store, being involved in youth ministry, and touring with the ballet company than I would have ever gotten had I attended public school. I am a happy, well-adjusted, outgoing adult, and given a choice, I wouldn't change anything about my life."

just no guarantee your child will be placed in one of those excellent situations. However, you might find that a private school will suit your needs just as well as homeschooling. After formulating the lists below, we based our decision to homeschool on what we preferred. Perhaps you should create a list of your own.

Homeschooling	Private School
One-on-one teaching	1:18 is average ratio
Learning is by retention	Learning is by repetition
Repeat what is missed	Move on or be left behind
Safety is assured	Safety is not guaranteed
Move at child's pace	Move at class's pace
Minimal costs	Monthly tuition

If I decide to homeschool, what subjects do I teach my child?

Your state will give you a list of the required courses for elementary, middle, and high school students. The list usually consists of English, mathematics, reading, spelling, social studies, and possibly health, physical education, and good citizenship. Each state has individual requirements. You're not limited to teaching just your state-required courses, but you may not omit or substitute any, either.

I've called HSLDA, received my state requirements, and will attend my first support group meeting tonight. Now what?

You're doing great! The next step would be to begin viewing different curricula for your child's needs, which we will discuss in chapter 4. You're not homeschooling if you pull your child from the public school without preparing some type of curriculum. Get in touch with a support group in your area; we can't say this enough. Its members are using a vast array of curricula and will be happy to discuss the advantages as well as the disadvantages of each. Look at several textbooks before making your purchase.

Where do I go to select a curriculum?

You don't have to go anywhere. Most selections can be made over the phone or the Internet, or by talking with other homeschoolers. This seemed like such a tough hurdle for us to cross when we first began. Don't let it be the same for you.

It's not the curriculum that produces a better student; it's the teaching methods.

The curriculum you choose for one child may not work for another. Read, research, and try different ones. And keep in mind that you can use one curriculum for math and another for language, for example. It isn't necessary to purchase what is called a "package" curriculum. Package curricula are wonderful if you find that all the subjects in the package are tailored to meet your child's needs. However, that is seldom the case. We found that purchasing each course separately works the best. In a classroom at a public or private school, a teacher is forced to use the same curriculum for everyone. This is not the case in homeschooling.

If you have joined a homeschooling support group, you're at an advantage. You've made friends with other home-schoolers who have curricula and definite opinions on what works and what doesn't. The support groups will also put you in touch with information on the next homeschooling convention, where

Don't fret about having the "perfect" curriculum.

the curriculum providers display their textbooks for your review. Go and visit the displays, even though you may not plan to attend the seminars at the conventions.

Our Curriculum Selection

When we were faced with selecting an appropriate curriculum, we didn't know if our children were visual learners, tactile learners, or another kind. Even if we had known, it wouldn't have mattered, because we didn't know how to evaluate a curriculum. So, we talked with other homeschooling parents and asked to look at their textbooks.

Although we didn't homeschool for religious purposes, when we first began we chose our language, mathematics, and science courses from Bob Jones University. As the year progressed, we became better equipped to make curriculum decisions based on each son's needs. For instance, the boys began to voice their opinions on what they wanted or needed in each course. They loved the science and mathematics courses for their clarity and visual perception. However, they found diagramming Bible verses extremely difficult in the language course. We agreed, and without even realizing it, we were evaluating curricula through trial and error.

You, too, may go through a trial-and-error period of selecting textbooks, supplemental courses, software, and video material, but don't fret over having the "perfect" course. It's not the curriculum that produces a better student; it's the teaching methods.

Where do I order textbooks and, more important, teacher's editions?

Let's say you have decided you don't need to join a support group, or there isn't one available in your area. You haven't been able to talk to another homeschooler about what textbooks she uses. And you're not on-line. Here is a brief list of curriculum suppliers to get started. This list encompasses secular and nonsecular textbooks.

Curriculum Providers

A Beka Book Publications, Box 18000, Pensacola, FL 32523-9160, 1-800-874-2352, http://www.abeka.com

Alpha Omega Publications, P.O. Box 3153, Tempe, AZ 85208, 1-800-622-3070, http://www.home-schooling.com

Alta Vista Curriculum, P.O. Box 55535, Seattle, WA 98155, 1-800-544-1397

Bob Jones University Press, Greenville, SC 29614,
1-800-845-5731, http://www.bju.edu

Bridgestone OnLine Academy, (877) 688-2652,
http://www.switchedonschoolhouse.com/bola

Calvert School, 105 Tuscany Rd., Baltimore, MD 21210,
(410) 243-6030, http://www.calvertschool.org

Cambridge Academy, 3300 SW 34th Ave., #102, Ocala, FL
34474, 1-800-252-3777

Christ-Centered Publications, P.O. Box 968, Tullahoma, TN
37388-0968, 1-800-884-7858

Christian Liberty Academy, 502 W. Euclid Ave., Dept. G,
Arlington Heights, IL 60004, 1-800-348-0899,
http://www.homeschools.org

Christian Light Education, P.O. Box 1212-N, Harrisonburg, VA
22801-1212, (540) 434-0750

Clonlara School, 1289 Jewett, Ann Arbor, MI 48104,
(313) 769-4515, http://www.grfn.org/education/clonlara

Curriculum Resource Center, P.O. Box 241, Dublin, NH 03444

Home Study International, 12501 Old Columbia Pike, Silver
Spring, MD 20904, 1-800-782-4769

Keystone National High School, 420 W. 5th St., Bloomsburg, PA
17815, 1-800-255-4937, http://www.keystonehighschool.
com

Laurel Springs School, 1002 E. Ojai Ave., P.O. Box 1440, Ojai,
CA 93024, (805) 646-2473, http://www.laurelsprings.com

Laurelwood Publications, Rt. 1, Box 87, Bluemont, VA 20135,
(540) 554-2670

Oak Meadow School, P.O. Box 740, Putney, VT 05346,
http://www.oakmeadow.com

Seton Home Study School, 1350 Progress Dr., Front Royal, VA
22630

Saxon Math, 1320 W. Lindsey, Norman, OK 73069,
1-800-646-6485

The Book Peddler, P.O. Box 1960, Elyria, OH 44036-1960,
1-800-928-1760, e-mail: TheBookPeddler@juno.com

Wilcox & Follet Book Co., 1000 W. Washington Blvd., Chicago, IL
60607, 1-800-621-4272

Used Textbooks

The Book Cellar, 189 Elm St., Milford, NH 03055,
1-800-338-4257, e-mail: bookcellar@juno.com

BUDGETexT Home Education, P.O. Box 1487, Fayetteville, AR
72702-1487, 1-888-888-2272,
e-mail: sales@homeschoolmall.com

Educators Exchange, 10755 Midlothian Tpk., Richmond, VA
23235, (804) 794-6994, e-mail: jscgec@aol.com

Homeschool Exchange, P.O. Box 1278, Boerne, TX 78006,
1-800-894-8247, e-mail: HSXchange@aol.com

Books That List Curriculum Providers

The Big Book of Home Learning: Preschool and Elementary, by
Mary Pride

The Big Book of Home Learning: Teen and Adult, by Mary Pride

Home Education Resource Guide, by Don Hubb

The Home School Source Book, by Donn Reed

Home Education Resource Guide, by Cheryl Gorder

Can I purchase the curriculum at a teacher's supply store or major bookstore?

Don't count on it. We found several supplemental workbooks at those types of stores, but not actual textbooks with teacher's editions. You may get lucky and find a book that you're happy with, but we didn't have much luck in the concentrated textbook department. We did find flash cards, charts, supplement workbooks, puzzles, educational games, and wonderful supplies.

Can I purchase textbooks from a college bookstore for my child?

Yes, some college bookstores carry elementary- and secondary-level textbooks intended for the college student majoring in education. Check out what is available at a college near you, and make sure to ask about the teacher's editions.

The Unschooling Method

I've heard of unschooling. What is that?

A growing number of homeschoolers are changing the way they think and becoming unschoolers. The best way to define unschooling, for there are several opinions, would be to say that the unschooling community is founded on the principle that children learn best when they pursue their individual interests. The unschooling movement is exploration of knowledge rather than textbook knowledge, which, in a way, is what homeschoolers additionally accomplish. However, since we didn't follow the methods of this movement, we're not the best people to define unschooling. Perhaps the following book would be of interest on this topic:

The Unschooling Handbook, How to Use the Whole World as Your Child's Classroom, by Mary Griffith

Some parents don't believe in using textbooks. Do I have to do so?

Although many unschoolers believe textbooks should not be used, we still recommend them. They were designed for educating. We used textbooks, swear by textbooks, and would be lost without them. It's very easy not to use textbooks if you have a child under the age of nine. It's another story getting a child into college if you profess never to have used a textbook.

I'd like to subscribe to a homeschooling magazine. Are any available?

There are several. The first homeschooling magazine we read was *Homeschooling Today.* It was a promotional issue from our state organization. Listed below are some others.

Homeschooling Periodicals

The Catholic Home Educator, P.O. Box 420225, San Diego, CA 92142

Home Education Magazine, P.O. Box 3142, Palmer, AK 99645-3142, 1-800-236-3278, http://www.home-ed-magazine.com

HomeSchool Dad Magazine, 609 Starlight Dr., Grand Junction, CO 81504, http://www.acsol.net/hsd

Homeschooling Today, P.O. Box 1425, Milrose, FL 32666, (904) 475-3088

The Link, 587 N. Ventu Park Rd., Suite F-911, Newbury Park, CA 91320, (805) 492-1373

National Homeschool Journal, P.O. Box 1372, Camono Island, WA 98292

Practical Homeschooling, P.O. Box 1250, Fenton, MO 63026, 1-800-346-6322

The Library

Does the library carry information about homeschooling?

Yes, but not always the most current information. We have a fairly new library in our area, yet most of its information on homeschooling is limited or somewhat outdated. Homeschooling tools have changed drastically in the last five years; verify copyright dates.

Some homeschooling support groups meet at the library, and they probably have more information about homeschooling than the library does. Our library even had a homeschooling bulletin board updated by homeschoolers. Ask your librarians what is available for homeschoolers; you'll find them most helpful. Every child, homeschooled or not, should have a library card.

In Summary

We know you still have many more questions that need to be answered. But you have gathered information on legal issues, support groups, and available curricula. We don't want to scare you off, so relax; it's not important that you contact every curriculum provider just yet. And don't schedule those private school interviews, either. Give us a chance to convince you that homeschooling could work for your family. There's so much more we have to tell you. Let's move on.

CHAPTER 2

It Just Takes a Little Confidence

Confidence in What You Can Achieve by Homeschooling

For years parents have been made to believe that certified teachers are the only people qualified to teach children. Parents begin to feel educationally inadequate when confronting teachers, administrators, or school officials because school jargon has taken on its own codes and labeling system. Add to that all the baggage we bring from our own school days. Sometimes schools mislabel children as having ADD (attention deficit disorder) or ADHD (attention deficit hyperactivity disorder), when all they really exhibit, at the most, is boredom. Throw in a few terms like "teaming" or "behavioral modification," and we parents become uncomfortable. We assume that if the teacher sounds as if he knows what he's talking about, he must be right. Thus, ultimately parents give up hope.

Dispel the Myth

Well, prospective homeschooler, it's time to dispel the myth that you aren't capable of educating your own child. Who knows your child better than you do? *Webster's World College Dictionary* defines *confidence* as belief in one's own abilities. It requires confidence to try new things, whether delivering a speech, obtaining your first driver's license, or considering homeschooling as an educational option. You're making a conscious effort to see what options homeschooling affords just by reading this book, and that's an excellent start.

> **Who knows your child better than you do?**

Perhaps you feel certain that you can teach your child without any problems during the primary years. It's just the high school years that intimidate you. Wherever your concerns may be focused, this chapter will elevate your level of confidence and assure you that homeschooling works tremendously well.

Am I qualified to teach my own child?

We're frequently asked this question, and it still aggravates us. Yes, you're qualified. Being the parent automatically qualifies you.

> **We learned that what we thought our children were getting as an education didn't meet our standards.**

Do you want your child to succeed in life? Do you find enjoyment in seeing your child develop mentally as well as physically? Do you want the best for your child? If you answered yes to all of these questions, then you will be fully capable of teaching your child. Only you can know what your child needs to succeed in life. If you are frustrated with the school system your child is currently enrolled in, then obviously something needs to be fixed, and you're accomplishing that by at least considering homeschooling.

Bypass the System

When our sons were given the interdistrict transfer, friends and relatives asked why we hadn't confronted the community by challenging the school board with demands for a better system, instead of choosing homeschooling. Why didn't we stand up and make some noise, write letters, contact the media?

At first, we did feel we should have fought harder, but while we might have been pursuing that effort, our children still would have been in the failing system. What would we have gained? We didn't want our children to be left behind while we directed our energies toward changing the system. If we were going to put forth any effort to fix things, it was going to be in teaching our children.

Life has a way of revealing itself through tragic events. We learned that the education we thought our children were receiving didn't meet our standards. Their fundamental skills in reading, mathematics, grammar, and spelling were low; so low, in fact, that our eighth grader read at a fifth grade level. We knew we had a big job ahead of us.

Time was of the essence. It was time to strengthen our children's educational skills, not time to complain about the system that our own government agrees isn't working properly. You see, homeschooling is fixing the problem right now. The nonfunctioning system is still out there, but our children bypassed it.

Yes, we've been criticized for bowing out of the system rather than putting forth a concentrated effort to make it better. Our first duty has always been to raise our children effectively. Although it's terrible to sit back and say, "Yes, the public schools are failing," doing nothing to help the current situation, we'll never be accused of neglecting our children's education. How's that for being qualified?

College Degrees and Teacher's Certification

Do I need a college degree to teach my child?

Some states require the child to be tutored by someone who

is certified, though certification need not mean a college degree in education.

There are certified teachers homeschooling their own children who confess certification didn't prepare them for teaching one-on-one. In fact, they felt having a degree in education hindered them at first because they were way too structured.

There is no proof that homeschoolers whose parents have college degrees score higher on yearly testing than homeschoolers whose parents don't have college degrees. It's the one-on-one training that prepares the child for the educational process. Face it: Everyone would learn better with a personal tutor. Think of yourself as your child's personal trainer.

HOPE: Home Oriented Private Education in Texas

Many parents are concerned that they are not certified teachers and won't have the skills necessary to teach their children. The handbook for Texas homeschoolers given out by Home Oriented Private Education (HOPE) states:

> Numerous research projects show that certification has no value in improving the educational results seen in the classroom. In fact, two studies indicated that certification was a negative influence. Research also shows very clearly that the educational background of the parents does not appreciably affect the student's academic accomplishments. Students taught by a parent with a high school diploma score almost exactly the same on standardized achievement tests as students taught by a parent with a graduate college degree. The major issue that determines the success of the student is the commitment of the teacher to see that the child learns the required subject. Committed teachers do whatever is necessary to modify the course to meet the needs of their students. No one can be more committed to a child than his own parents.

We certainly agree with that.

Why Choose Homeschooling?

Is it okay to homeschool my child because I'm afraid for his safety in a public school?

It's okay to homeschool your child for whatever reason you deem necessary. You won't have to fill out a form stating your reasons for homeschooling. As you meet more parents who've chosen homeschooling as an alternative to public education, you'll realize that every parent expresses a different concern or reason to homeschool. Believe in your convictions for homeschooling, whatever the reason. And don't let anyone tell you your reasons aren't valid enough to homeschool.

Why do most families choose homeschooling?

We've met wonderful and interesting families from all walks of life with unique reasons for homeschooling. Yet, though everyone had different reasons for choosing homeschooling, homeschoolers share a common bond of commitment. We are passionate about educating our own children. We simply feel we can do a better job of teaching our children than anyone else.

Other Parents' Stories

"My child needed individual attention when it came to learning a new task, because her mind wandered. She was getting left behind in the private school."

"Our child was afraid to go to school. He had been in several fights and had his winter coat taken from him. You can't expect a child to learn in an environment that's frightening."

"Our child didn't do well in the open classroom concept. He didn't focus on just what his teacher was saying. He listened to all the teachers in his work area, which led to confusion."

"My child is handicapped. Even in the special education classes the ratio of students to teacher was high. He needed individual attention in so many subjects."

"My child wanted to pursue a skating career and homeschooling was the perfect choice. We can homeschool without the stress of having to rush through our work to make skating practice."

"I noticed my child brought home nothing but busywork. When were the schools going to get down to the basics? I stepped in and started teaching him how to read and spell while he attended public school. It took me almost a year before I realized he was going to school to play and coming home to learn."

"We prepared our child for school beyond what a first grader needed to know. Despite the fact she was in the gifted and talented program, she was bored the first month of school and began to develop behavior problems. The school informed us that she knew too much for her grade level and labeled her hyperactive."

"Our son had no respect for teachers, family, or himself. Homeschooling at his pace corrected his self-esteem problems, which in turn made him more respectful of others."

"Our family is transferred every few years, making the adjustment to new schools a bit difficult for our children. Homeschooling made life less stressful for our family and put us in touch with support groups of caring families."

"My children's education was lacking a moral content. They brought home homework that dealt with stories and poems about gang problems, suicide thoughts, and drug-dealing parents. We felt there was so much more they could have studied that reflected a positive outlook on life."

"Our child couldn't read well in the sixth grade and the school kept passing him with A's."

"My son never learned how to sound out words; consequently he didn't read or spell well at all. He had been taught inventive spelling. What was that?"

"We never remembered our parents having to work with us on homework as much as we had to with our children. We were already reteaching what they hadn't understood during the day at school. Why send them to public school? We were their schoolteachers!"

"We just got tired of being frustrated with the system. The schools say they want parental involvement, but they mean in cutting out bulletin board decorations. It was ridiculous how many math concepts our children didn't do properly. When we wrote notes to the teachers, they told our children not to worry, the concept would be explained in next year's class."

Dropout Homeschoolers

What about the children who are dropouts pretending to homeschool?

What about those teenagers who had problems in the public or private sector and dropped out of school, and their parents profess they are homeschooling? You've heard those parents say, "Oh, Tim works on the Internet on his studies. He is self-taught." You've seen Tim outside on the front porch smoking and hanging out with his buddy dropouts. Tim has even fooled his parents into thinking this is homeschooling.

That is a dropout, not a homeschooler. He is no different from the teenager who sleeps in class at a public school. You just don't see the one who is asleep. He gets away with saying he's getting an education, but is he? There will always be somebody who abuses the system.

The Law and the School System

Here is how the law and school work in simple terms. In the United States, education is compulsory. This means that, by law, children must attend school a required number of days per year for a certain number of years. The number of years and the grade levels a child must finish vary from one state to another.

If a child is ill and cannot attend regular classes at school, the state must permit her to have an alternative education. Some schools are required to provide alternative education. If alternative education is decided upon, such as homeschooling, there are restrictions. The parents must truly be teaching their children, not merely saying they will educate their children when they have no intention of doing so. Children who do not attend school are considered truants in the eyes of the law. Truant officers investigate students' absences from school. Leave it up to the truant officers to handle the dropouts that hide behind the homeschooling laws.

Grandma, Tom, Dick, and Harry

What will our friends and relatives have to say?

First of all, you shouldn't care. They're not responsible for raising your child. You are. But that advice doesn't make it any easier for you when your mother or your sister challenges your motives with the following questions:

What about sports, school dances, and cheerleading?

Isn't that for the scary religious people?

What about their social life?

Why would you want to teach your own children?

How can you have your career if you have to worry about your children?

Isn't it the school's job to teach them?

We handled our friends and relatives by expressing, in no uncertain terms, that we were asking for their support, not their advice. When they asked us questions we couldn't answer, we simply admitted we were taking one day at a time. You'll have an easier time; remember, this book wasn't available for us. Your friends' and relatives' questions are sure to be answered throughout this book, so maybe you'll want to read it before you hold that family meeting.

Don't be too upset by what others base a good education on, like dances and football games. After a short time of homeschooling, you'll hear those same people give you credit for undertaking such a worthwhile project. Grandma and Grandpa will be bragging about your homeschooling techniques and success at the next family reunion. You'll learn to disregard those people who have doubts about your abilities. They're really evaluating whether they would be able to be as dedicated to the task as you. When people challenged us by asking why we would ever want to homeschool, it was easier to respond, "Why wouldn't we?"

Social Skills

We address social concerns throughout this book, because they are a big factor to consider when choosing to homeschool your child, especially in the teen years. Don't confuse peer social skills, however, with general social skills. Social skills are learned in the home first. Believe it or not, you have a lot to do with your child's social character and abilities.

When was the last time you had a conversation with a teenager you met? Take a good look at the teenagers today. They have a difficult time carrying on a conversation with an adult without staring at their shoes or shifting from foot to foot in disinterest. Have a conversation with a homeschooled child. He looks you in the eye, shakes your hand, and carries on an intelligent conversation.

Our children were the first to notice that homeschooling gave them confidence in their self-worth. They admitted that they felt intelligent enough to convey their opinions when talking to adults.

We taught them to ask questions and gave them the will to want to learn more. A homeschooler can cuddle a small child, talk with students her own age about the newest trends, and converse with adults about a current event with the greatest of ease. What better socializing could there possibly be?

A Much-Debated Topic of Interest

Social concerns are a much-debated issue between the homeschooling community and the general public. There are plenty of surveys to show that homeschoolers have nothing to worry about in the social department, but they are just statistics. Each child is different.

MARC KIDWELL

"During my homeschooling experience, I was repeatedly told by others that I would not be able to function in the 'real world.' People stated that since I didn't have the experience of a public high school, I would lack the social skills necessary to succeed in a college classroom or in the workplace. My family members were considered right-wing radicals. What others didn't realize was the dedication my parents put forth to offer the best education for both me and my sister brought our family closer together. In fact, I have a relationship with my mother and father that is envied by many of my peers."

Marc Kidwell smiles when he remembers his homeschooling days during the mid-'80s, at a time when very few people in Ohio were attempting this form of education. It was a time when the general public assumed homeschoolers would become socially repressed. He tells us, "Homeschooling isn't for everyone. Homeschooling won't work without the presence of discipline and a set schedule. My parents made sure that school started every day at 8:15 with a set course schedule. This included physical education,

The Extrovert

There are children who join every homeschooling group or event, play in Little League, or become Girl Scouts. Homeschooling will afford them the concentrated time they need to focus on academics during the day. Extracurricular activities in the afternoon will provide the socializing they need to become well-rounded persons. They will remain well adjusted and benefit greatly from the one-on-one education.

The Introvert

Then, of course, there are homeschoolers who are shy and don't join extracurricular activities. It'll be up to the parent to make sure that socializing becomes part of the home education.

music, and computer training. Too often, I hear of homeschool situations where the students are allowed to sleep until noon and complete class work when they 'get around to it.' I believe that my success after homeschooling was the result of the discipline and routine taught by my parents.

"After homeschooling, college and the workforce are a piece of cake. The entire time I was in college, I kept waiting for it to get more difficult. The discipline and work ethic that my parents had instilled in me through homeschooling are what set me apart from everyone else."

Marc received an A.A. degree from Eastern Christian College, a B.A. from Lincoln Christian College, and soon will begin work on his M.A. He is currently the minister of Youth and Christian Education at the Smyrna Church of Christ, where he is responsible for teacher training, curriculum, and supervision of the educational program. Prior to this he held a position in the performance development and improvement department of a major bank. Marc's goals include sharing the Gospel, raising a family with his wife, and eventually teaching at the collegiate level.

However, in regard to public education, we ask you to consider an important factor. Just because a child sits in a classroom full of children his own age doesn't mean he'll have someone to play with at recess or sit with at lunch. If you have concerns about the socialization of your child, make sure to provide adequate opportunities to join extracurricular activities.

My child and I don't get along. Is homeschooling for us?

There are plenty of people who say they could never teach their own children without yelling. They're sure their children wouldn't listen. If you're arguing over your son's nose ring or haircut to the point of frustration and yelling, maybe you should rethink homeschooling.

> **If you're yelling at each other, you can't learn together.**

It's a must that you have a good relationship with your child, regardless of whether you homeschool or not. Homeschooling will bring you closer if you truly listen to the needs of your children. You'll learn to pinpoint what skills they're lacking after a little while of teaching and working with them. Don't just tell them they're lacking the skills, though; fix the problem. As you begin to work on those skills you'll develop a wonderful relationship with your children, making them feel proud of themselves. Maybe your son will forget about getting the nose ring, or you'll get one with him.

We still believe that we weren't the teachers and the children weren't the students. We shared both roles, learning together. If you're yelling at each other, you can't learn together. Having homeschooled our children, we got to repeat our high school education, and the children truly received an education, but together, we developed respect for each other.

Are homeschooled children different from other children?

Many homeschooling families would say yes, but we would

have to say no. Kids are kids no matter whether they're home-schooled, public schooled, or private schooled. There are polite homeschoolers and polite public school students, just as there are rude homeschoolers and rude public school students. To make the broad statement that homeschooled children are different from other children would be wrong.

We tutor public and private schooled children who are very much like our children. They have hopes, dreams, failures, and successes. When given the opportunity to express themselves in a nurtured, nonthreatening environment, they all have the desire to learn.

Do you admit that public and private schools aren't educating students as well as they could?

We have nothing against the educators and superintendents of public and private schools in America. They have one of the toughest and most stressful jobs in this country.

Education in America is failing, no doubt, but it's a combination of several factors, including and not limited to families falling apart, moral decline, teacher burnout, underpaid educators, financially poor school districts, and safety problems. We aren't saying that children

> **If the school system isn't living up to your expectations; if your child needs one-on-one tutoring help; if you want to correct the problem right now; then you, nobody else, must fix the problem.**

in a public or private school won't get a good education. What we're saying, though, is that you, as the parent, should monitor what they're learning to make sure they're not missing the essentials. It might not be fair that you have to assume this responsibility, but it's a fact.

Right now, homeschooling is fixing that problem for many families. If you feel you can keep your child in the public or private sector and continually monitor her education, making sure your standards are being maintained, then that is fixing the problem just as effectively.

Can I get a refund on my property tax from the school system to which I don't send my child?

Hardly! Despite the fact that you'll still pay property taxes for a school your child won't attend, you can't receive a refund. Perhaps you should call your government officials and make some noise about the situation.

Can I use a voucher for education to help with the expenses of homeschooling?

Don't wait around for voucher proposals to be given to homeschoolers. Charter schools and vouchers take money away from the public schools, and the public schools probably wouldn't look kindly on the homeschooling community if it received voucher opportunities. But there's nothing saying you can't fight to change that.

I've heard about the bill called Education Savings Accounts. What is it?

Education Savings Accounts is a proposed federal bill that would allow parents to set aside money in interest-bearing savings accounts to use for education expenses. It hasn't passed as of this writing.

Homeschooling on a Budget

Is it expensive to homeschool?

Well, if you plan on touring every country that you study, it could be costly. As a matter of fact, we know of one such homeschooling family that had the luxury of taking a year to tour the world. Wouldn't it be wonderful if every family could learn history, geography, and art by visiting many countries?

Homeschooling can be as inexpensive or expensive as you choose it to be. We saved money by not having to shop for school clothes. Without the peer pressure, designer label clothing takes a backseat to sweatpants and T-shirts. Backpacks, school lunches, and gym shoes aren't as important, either.

On a more realistic note, books from most curriculum sellers range from $10 to $90 each, with teacher's editions being slightly higher. If you have more than one child, you'll probably use your books more than once. Take advantage of the opportunity to purchase used books from local support groups. There will always be a market for used books as homeschooling grows. Your money will be spent on school supplies, possibly lab experiment supplies, or a home computer system.

Those homeschoolers who have spent more than they would have liked attribute it to trial and error. We have purchased courses for our children that didn't fit our needs. This was because we didn't do our research, but bought impulsively. We're sure you'll learn from our mistakes. Pretty packaging doesn't mean effective teaching tools.

Ways to Save Money on Homeschooling Supplies

Visit garage sales, thrift shops, and library book sales and look for books, Lego's, puzzles, board games, flash cards, and other useful items. We even found our son's graduation cap and gown at a garage sale, sealed in plastic. After we casually remarked to the owner that it was a shame that the gown had been a one-time purchase, one-time-worn item, he replied, "Yeah, a waste of money for sure. My son didn't even graduate. He never passed the exit exam from high school." Enough said.

For more information, see *Homeschooling on a Shoestring: A Complete Guide to Options, Strategies, Resources, and Costs*, by Melissa L. Morgan.

How will I know when I've purchased enough books on the subject of homeschooling?

We still purchase books having to do with homeschooling even though our oldest has graduated from college and is now working. Laws change. New material comes to the market. Keep shopping for new ideas and trends in the education of your child.

It Will Take Energy

I just don't know if I could keep it up day after day.

Then homeschooling may not be for you. We said this book would be straightforward on the answers. It's an ongoing project to educate your child. If you're frustrated with the school your child is attending, but don't feel homeschooling is for you, it's time to consider different options. Maybe you want private school instead of public school. Maybe you need a tutor who can work with your child once a week. Maybe you could homeschool one or two

HANNAH BOWYER

"There are so many benefits to homeschooling, but one of the best from my perspective was the one-on-one attention. As my mom grew confident in homeschooling, she was able to design her own curriculum tailor-made to my needs. She didn't teach for 'tests' but taught me how to learn the material.

"My first year of college, although I did well academically, was a rough adjustment socially and very stressful, although some of this might have been due to my young age and deciding 'who I was.' My recommendation to others who have homeschooled from kindergarten through grade twelve would be to either start off in a Christian college or go to a Christian high school to help make the adjustment easier."

At sixteen, Hannah Bowyer was the youngest full-time student to enroll at Darton College in Albany, Georgia, where she was on the dean's list, served on the Student Government Association, was the vice president of the Baptist Student Union, and was in *Who's Who in American Junior Colleges.* She was also given the honor of being selected as a Darton Ambassador, a small group of students days a week after school to make sure your child is keeping up. Weigh the options.

We know of one couple who felt their child needed tutoring but also admitted that they were unable to meet that need. Teaching their own child made them frustrated, yet they had the patience of a saint teaching others. They made a flyer for the school bulletin board offering to trade tutoring skills with another family and were contacted by a family that had been looking for the very same thing. It worked out just fine, helping to solve the situation for both families.

Do I have to stay at home for the entire day with my children?

Homeschoolers don't necessarily spend their entire day sitting

recommended by the faculty to represent the college to accreditation committees, to other schools, at college fairs, and in television commercials and newspaper ads.

Hannah's parents chose homeschooling because they didn't have transportation to the Christian school of their choice. Hannah's mother saw an advertisement for a curriculum available to missionary children and resolved to research homeschooling. She decided to give homeschooling a try for kindergarten. Twenty years later Hannah's mother, considered a pioneer of homeschooling in her hometown, continues to homeschool Hannah's siblings.

Hannah and her husband, Ron, have two young children whom they plan on homeschooling. Hannah is the assistant manager of a Web site for homeschooling mothers, which can be reached at the following URL:

http://communities.msn.com/ProjectTitus2/homepage

Hannah says she is truly grateful to her parents for their time and effort in homeschooling her, and that she is very proud to be a homeschooled graduate.

at the kitchen table working on their courses, although sometimes we did exactly that. We would get into a project, and time would get away from us. Before we knew it, we had worked the entire day on our studies. However, homeschoolers do have to grocery shop, go to the doctor, run errands, and do normal household chores. We got up early, did our schoolwork, and still had plenty of time to run errands and join extracurricular activities.

It needs to be said, however, that if you don't enjoy sharing time with your child, then the homeschooling experience may not be what you're looking for as alternative education. Homeschooling is a family experience. Homeschooling takes place no matter where you locate. There were days that we packed up our books and spent the day at the beach reading and fishing. Schooling took place on camping trips to the desert. We felt that was every bit as much homeschooling as sitting at our kitchen table all day long reviewing lessons.

Negatives of Homeschooling

Could you give me the negatives of homeschooling?

Everyone should have all the facts about an endeavor before beginning; however, our negatives about homeschooling may not be your negatives. Nevertheless, many negatives can become positives if they're looked at from a new perspective.

You're responsible for educating your child fully. There will be nobody else to blame. If your child can't read or perform simple mathematical problems, it's your fault. (No pressure!)

Although most homeschoolers score very high on their college admission tests, it's essential that they do well on the SAT. Some colleges have a higher SAT score acceptance level for the homeschooler to meet.

Sometimes, homeschoolers have problems entering the military without a diploma or GED. The Air Force Academy accepted a female homeschooler in 1999. This is a definite advance in the acceptance of homeschoolers by the military, probably due to the fact that there are many military families homeschooling their children.

You, as the main teacher, will experience burnout at least a few times along the way. You'll have days of frustration, anxiety, and less patience at times.

It's harder to obtain athletic scholarships than if your child were in public or private schools. You need to do the recruiting for your child who possesses athletic talents. You're the coach, administration, and recruiter.

Homeschoolers need to actively pursue extracurricular activities, sometimes leading to traveling great distances. (You need to drive them to the social activities.)

When your child goes off to college, you may experience the blues more than is normal, having spent more time with your child than most parents. Then again, you may jump for joy.

As the main homeschooling parent, you may experience the need for time alone. This has to do with burnout.

If priorities are not in place, you'll face the stress of living on only one income. You need to learn to live on a budget.

You may feel guilty taking a sick day. You can assign lessons for your children, but they still might need your help, especially if they're young. It's rather hard to climb into bed with the flu and tell your child to do his schoolwork.

It's extremely hard to have a career that involves most of your time if you choose to homeschool. One parent will probably have to hold down a full-time job. This isn't to say single-income families are the only ones homeschooling. You might have to hire a tutor to homeschool your child if you choose to continue with a full-time career.

And, this is a tough one to admit, but you may have to purchase reading glasses. (Or you can choose to grow longer arms.)

Part-Time Homeschooling

Can I homeschool my child and send her to a public or private school?

Sure; it's called tutoring your child, and we discuss this in depth in chapter 3. Asian Americans have been tutoring their children in addition to sending them to public school for years. They've had the right idea all along. What their children don't understand at school, the parents explain at home.

You can order curricula to enhance your child's education and work on his weak fundamentals. If your whole objective is to educate your child more efficiently, then this will work most effectively. The tough part is when your child is bogged down with busywork from the public school and has no energy to work on the skills you feel need attention.

Can I send my child to public or private schools for one class, such as a foreign language or physical education class, but homeschool the rest of the courses?

It never hurts to contact your school district office and ask. Homeschooling parents are actively seeking permission for their children to join public and private school athletic programs. It will depend upon your working relationship with your school district.

This is a much-debated topic with homeschoolers and public schools. It probably won't be long before more school districts adopt this policy of allowing homeschoolers to participate in foreign language courses or even athletics, if the school districts can work out the state funding situation.

Reentering Public or Private School After Homeschooling a Few Years

We placed our youngest son back in the public school system for his high school years. Socially, he was shy. We expected it would take a period of adjustment for him to make new friends. He met his share of students that were rude and obnoxious, and he was told by several of his peers that he was too polite to be a teenager. He may have had to toughen up a bit, but he adjusted just fine, despite the fact that he is still a nice guy!

Academically, he soared above the others and possessed a level of confidence he had never before experienced in his academic skills. One of the things he expressed was that he wasn't afraid to talk with his teachers, ask questions, or give his opinion. He carried his homeschooling social skills back into the public school classroom.

Most of his teachers were surprised at how well he related to them with confidence on an equal or one-on-one basis. After about a month, we received compliments on his attitude from teachers, peers, and administrators. They said, "We can tell he is a home-schooled student, for he is extremely confident and polite when expressing his opinions." That, we thought, is a wonderful com-pliment for the entire homeschooling community. Sometimes, homeschooling for a year or two is just what a student needs to excel in the public or private schools today. Everyone could use a confidence booster, and it doesn't hurt to have an academic booster, as well.

Discussing the Negatives

Again, we stress that our negatives about reentering the public or private school system may not be your negatives, and that most negatives work themselves out eventually.

Your child might not be able to work at the same pace as her class after having been allowed to work at an individual one. Our son complained there was never enough time to finish his work to his satisfaction. His teachers felt his work was above average. He felt rushed. Therefore, it wasn't his best.

Your child may have an adjustment period of learning how to take a test. Many homeschooling parents don't create tests for their children to take. Therefore, the child hasn't had the pressure of passing a test. This was a tough one for our son. He knew the material, but couldn't take the test quickly. You'll need to meet with your child's teachers and make them aware of this situation.

Your child may feel that some of the assignments are busy-work and not learning techniques.

Your child may be a bit shy making friends, especially in the middle school and high school years.

Your child will have to learn how to get along with different teachers, have scheduled lunch and bathroom breaks, raise her hand to ask questions, and let other classmates answer questions, too!

Conflict with a Teacher

Our youngest son, Jeff, was enrolled in an advanced English class that required a great deal of writing. He is a writer at heart, though he chooses to be a golfer at heart. His English teacher, a very wise and proficient educator, accused him of not doing his own work.

She kept him after class one day and tried to get him to admit that he hadn't written a particular summary of a story they had read in class, insisting the quality was beyond the high school level. Of course he didn't tell her that he had been a homeschooler and had taken every writing course his mother could get her hands on. He assured the teacher that he had indeed done his own work. She asked him to explain how he wrote the summary, which he did. Still a bit suspicious, she reluctantly gave him an A, not for the actual summary, but because he thoroughly explained how he derived the information necessary to write the summary.

Our son, with a mischievous grin on his face, couldn't wait to share what took place at school. After he did, we contacted the teacher and made her aware of his writing abilities and homeschooling experience. She apologized the moment we mentioned the word *homeschooling* and admitted she should have guessed. She now takes more time with our son and endlessly enters his writing pieces in essay contests. He's not too thrilled with us!

Sharing the Homeschooling Responsibility

Will my spouse and I equally share the homeschooling responsibility?

If your question is related to "at all times," the answer is no. In our home, 80 percent of the teaching was conducted by Mom and 20 percent by Dad. With Dad carrying the full-time job needed to run the family and household, homeschooling by him wouldn't have been possible. That is every bit of sharing the homeschooling responsibility.

At our wedding a grandmother of ours told us that marriage is sharing. She said, "Both of you will have to give and take. Just keep in mind, sometimes one will give 90 percent and the other will give 10 percent. Don't try and keep score in your marriage; it breeds arguments." She was a wonderfully wise grandmother. That is a good slogan for homeschooling, too. Don't try to keep score on who is teaching the children more.

Mom, if you're doing most of the teaching while your husband works full-time, thank him every day for the opportunity. Dad, if you're doing most of the teaching while your wife works full-time, thank her for the opportunity. No matter what, Mom and Dad, each of you should actively ask your children what they learned every day.

Can I hire someone to homeschool my child?

As long as you're within state guidelines, then yes; families do this quite often. Grandmothers are homeschooling. Aunts and uncles are homeschooling. Mothers are sharing knowledge. Those who have talents in a particular subject such as art or music are giving classes in their homes or local churches for interested homeschoolers. Some mothers are homeschooling other children for extra income. Taking on another family's child can also help with the social interaction of your children.

Grandma and Grandpa in on the Action

Our children's ninety-two-year-old great-grandfather, Great Poppy, came to visit twice a year, bringing stories of the Great Depression and Babe Ruth. Our boys would listen for hours while Great Poppy shared firsthand knowledge. Those hours listening to him beat all the textbooks put together. Many of those hours in which our children were receiving their history education from Great

Poppy were spent on the golf course playing a round of golf together. Now, we ask you, is there any better way to homeschool than that?

A grandparent is the perfect person to teach your child how to tell time, read a map, or count money. A grandparent will be happy to listen to your child recite the list of presidents or even the Gettysburg Address.

The boys' grandpa stood on a ladder painting the family room walls, listening to the boys learning the list of presidents. From the top of the ladder, Sonny Papa began reciting: "Washington, Adams, Jefferson . . ." The boys were astonished at what Grandpa remembered. "Once memorized, never forgotten," Papa boasted with authority. Never turn a grandparent's help away; it will give you a break to catch up on something you haven't had time to do, like take a bath.

Quick Results

Will I see results quickly?

When we first began homeschooling we would ask our children if they understood the lesson we were teaching. They would nod yes, and we would move on. It wasn't until the next lesson that we realized they really hadn't understood the previous lesson at all. When we asked them why they responded with a nod of assurance, they replied, "Well, I didn't understand it then, but I figured I'd get it eventually."

They learned that attitude in the public schools. Education for the masses leaves behind those who don't ask questions and demand answers. It'll take awhile to break your children's habit of pretending they understand a lesson when they truly don't. They've attended schools where peer pressure dictated whether they were given the opportunity to ask questions freely without ridicule.

Correspondence Schools/ Umbrella Programs

What is an umbrella program?

Parents can enroll their children in a correspondence, satellite, or private school that provides a fully prepared curriculum along with teacher's guides, testing, support, and record keeping. It's a unique idea, and the service costs less than the full private school program. These programs are very helpful for beginners who may be a bit intimidated by the idea of creating tests, report cards, and transcripts on their own.

Ask your curriculum provider if it furnishes an umbrella or satellite program. A few are listed below. For a concentrated list of umbrella/correspondence schools, you might wish to purchase the book *Home Education Resource Guide* by Cheryl Gorder. It's an excellent resource guide, complete with descriptions of what each school has to offer.

Home Study International, 1-800-782-4769

Indiana University Independent Study, 1-800-334-1011

Seton Home Study School, 1350 Progress Dr., Fort Royal, VA 22630

Summit Christian Academy, 1-800-362-9180

University of Nebraska at Lincoln, (402) 472-4321

University of Missouri Center for Independent Study, 1-800-609-3727

Texas Tech University, P.O. Box 42191, Lubbock, TX 79409-2191

Let's Hear from the Children

What do children like and dislike about homeschooling?

We polled a group of homeschoolers to make a list of what they liked and disliked about homeschooling, being careful to include children who had been in a public school before or after they homeschooled. Here are their comments:

Likes: Flexible school hours; fewer school hours; individual attention; working at their own pace; repeating lessons that were not understood; no excessive homework; many field trips; freedom to get up and walk around when necessary; ability to homeschool outside; no punishment for other classmates' actions.

Dislikes: Teens missed not having enough sports or clubs to join and missed seeing friends throughout the day. Some didn't like year-round homeschooling. Some young homeschoolers missed riding the bus.

Mature Beyond Their Years

Do we encourage homeschoolers to mature faster than their peers?

Well, that varies. Some homeschoolers feel they have matured faster than their peers because they have learned to communicate their thoughts in a more adult fashion. We homeschooled with the intention of preparing our children for college, career, and life. To us, that meant they needed to learn excellent communication skills to achieve what they wanted in life. It also meant that writing, reading, and speaking were priorities in our education plan. They had their share of fun, but they also learned there was a time for learning and a time for playing.

> "My seven-year-old finished calculus. My five-year-old speaks fluent French."

Pushing a Child

Homeschooling parents seem to be pushing their children to learn. Is that the case?

Homeschooling parents are involved in the education of their children, so they tend to be absorbed in the newest educational textbooks, methods, supplements, and whatever is available for their children. They are parents with a passion for teaching and learning. They want their children to succeed just like other parents do. So, as homeschooling parents, we tend to talk about our children's educational leaps and bounds. This might just be bragging on our part, not necessarily pushing.

Do families homeschool differently based on what they feel is most important?

There are definitely different degrees and levels of homeschooling. As you begin to associate with homeschooling families you'll discover that each one places emphasis on a particular course. Some move at an easy pace, with no particular goal of completing a specific course in one school year. Others move rapidly through their courses, completing more than one grade level in a given year. Both would be considered appropriate ways to homeschool.

Always teach at your child's pace.

We placed an emphasis on reading, literature, creative writing, and mathematics. After a few months of homeschooling you'll emphasize individual courses for your child's interests, too.

Do homeschooling parents worry whether they're covering enough material in a school year?

Some of us, usually beginner homeschooling parents, wonder whether we're covering each course in enough detail. Because it's the parents' responsibility to see that the child is learning, we tend to be critical of our abilities and ourselves. This usually happens with the first child who is homeschooled since we feel inexperienced at the task. Once homeschooling parents have about a year or two under their belts, they tend to relax and slow down the lesson plans. At first, it's quite normal to feel that you have "so much" to cover. If you teach at your child's pace, you'll stay on track.

Will I be sheltering my child from real life?

Homeschooling is real life today.

Homeschooling is real life today. Homeschooling does provide a controlled environment for your child to learn in, one that is safe and free of stress. Don't public and private schools control the child's environment as well? The key factor is that the home will provide a relaxed environment, one in which it is easier to learn.

When we were asked if we thought we were sheltering our children, we simply answered yes. They weren't bullied, teased, criticized, or made fun of during their day. They became eager to learn, aware of others' feelings, and consequently compassionate human beings. What was wrong with that? We taught them that the world could be cruel, and they would find rude people. We just made sure none of those people were in our home to stop the process of learning the skills necessary for life.

One- or Two-Income Families

Can both parents work, or does homeschooling require one parent to be at home?

Both parents can work, but one parent needs to be present while the homeschooling takes place. A child doesn't homeschool alone.

The beauty of homeschooling is the schedule flexibility. Parents can share the homeschooling responsibilities. We chose to live on one income, giving us the traditional one parent staying home during the day. It worked for us. However, some lessons were saved for the evening hours when Dad was available. This is a team effort of learning. Where there's a will, there's a way.

The Single Parent

I'm a single parent considering homeschooling, but what do I do with my child while I'm at work during the day?

We have never heard anyone answer this question directly. If you work during the day, it wouldn't be appropriate to let your child watch television or play outside alone until you got home. And we don't feel it would be appropriate to let your child learn his studies alone, without you. That's not homeschooling. However, we have visited with single parents who successfully homeschool their children by maintaining a flexible work schedule in and out of the home.

Maybe you need to consider the reasons you wish to homeschool. If you're homeschooling because you don't feel that your child is safe at school, and you have her home working on the computer until you return, that might not be a benefit to the child. If you're homeschooling because your child was expelled from school, but he is watching television all day, that's not homeschooling, either. Maybe you need to think about homeschooling as a supplement after the day at school, or about getting a tutor. If you're waiting for the homeschooling community to tell you it's okay to let your child lie around until you get home, you might find us reluctant to acknowledge that as homeschooling.

Chores to Do

How will I keep up with my housework if my child is home?

You won't, so don't sweat it. If you live in a house that looks as if it could be on the cover of a decorating magazine, taking all your energy to keep the house that way, homeschooling will soon become your new priority in life. Educating your child for life will take precedence over vacuuming, flash cards over dusting, and the Pythagorean theorem over mopping the floor. Learn to let the small stuff go. (Isn't there a cute little incentive book entitled *Don't Sweat the Small Stuff*? Maybe you should pick up a copy.)

Teach your family members to pick up after themselves and be more responsible. Make this a family living course. We know homeschoolers who set aside two hours each week in a joint effort to clean house. It won't hurt today's kids to learn how to pitch in.

Homeschooling and the Law

You tell me I need to know the state laws about homeschooling, but to tell the truth, I don't understand all that legal jargon. Is it explained in terms I'll understand?

Yes. When you contact your state organization or join HSLDA, it will provide you with your state's requirements or tell you how to obtain a copy of them. They are self-explanatory. Read them, know them. If you haven't called your state organization, turn to the back of this handbook and get your state organization's number. Even if you decide not to homeschool, you can still get on the homeschooling mailing lists.

As the parent/teacher, will I feel overwhelmed at times?

Yes. Plain and simple, you'll be undertaking a big job educating your child. When our children were in public school, the school sent a memo home for all the parents.

It read as follows:

It's the school's job to teach the child.
It's the parent's job that the child learns.
The school accepts no responsibility for your child learning.

We were appalled at such a blatant statement from the school, but after thinking it over, we saw that it's very true. We pinned the statement on our bulletin board as an incentive to keep homeschooling. It is our job that our children learn.

Take one day at a time. There's no hurry. On the days we felt most stressed, we had been trying to accomplish too much. The bell won't ring during one of your lessons. You won't have to practice fire drills during your school day; at least, we hope you won't. Just as a job can become overwhelming, so can homeschooling. The rewards are so much better, though. Remember, you and your child can take time out to have lemonade together when the stress level is mounting. Isn't homeschooling wonderful?

Homeschooling at the Beach

On one particular day we began work on our algebra lessons. It was a nice rainy day, the kind of day that makes you feel cozy being inside a warm house while it drizzles outside. We played soft classical music in the background while we worked on factoring algebra problems. We had a pizza in the oven that smelled heavenly.

At about that time the dog decided to christen the dining room carpet with a downright nasty case of diarrhea. But that wouldn't hinder us from our cozy day; no sir, we were dedicated homeschoolers. We cleaned up the mess, lit a few candles (okay, several vanilla-scented candles), and shoved the dog outside. It was back to algebra and a burned pizza.

About a half hour later we learned that the toilet had overflowed, the washing machine never had spun out, and the kitchen sink was backing up. We couldn't take any more that day trying to hold our noses while doing math problems.

We packed up our schoolbooks and drove to the beach. Schoolwork that day was done from the back of our Explorer while overlooking the waves crashing at the shore. Yes, it was raining, but ask us if we cared. No! It was the best creative writing day we ever had. So, it started out stressful, but it ended happily.

The job of educating your child should not be looked upon lightly, but it shouldn't be all serious stuff, either. Each family will define its own role. The trick will be in keeping a sense of humor. In our family, we found listening intently to each other worked wonders. The occasional dinner out without our children didn't hurt, either. Stay interested in the little things life has to offer and be in awe of each other's abilities.

The family of homeschoolers that lives down the block seems nice, but their home and yard look so disorganized. Are all homeschoolers so disorganized?

We smile at this question. What appears to be organized for one family isn't for another, but we understand what you mean. In homeschooling families, family and educational needs come first, not cutting the grass. That's not to say all homeschoolers have terrible-looking yards. As a matter of fact, our yard is beautiful. It's the inside of the garage that's a disaster.

As you get active in the homeschooling movement you'll find that you have less time for the little things. Educating your child will be your first priority, not trimming hedges. Nevertheless, there are some homeschoolers who put us all to shame. They have perfectly manicured lawns and immaculate houses, perfectly dressed little ones, washed cars, and time to sip iced tea on the back patio. Some people are just well organized.

How Secretive Should You Be About Homeschooling?

Should I be secretive about homeschooling my child?

Think about this for a moment. Why don't you want others to know that you homeschool? Look back to your list of concerns. You have to homeschool without being afraid to look over your shoulder. The only possible reason you should have to fear homeschooling would be not understanding the legalities of your particular state. So take the time to learn them. Follow your state's requirements, and don't worry about what others think. This is your child who needs to be educated.

We never tried to hide the fact that we were homeschoolers, but we confess we didn't volunteer the information freely when we first began. After about a year of homeschooling and meeting more people who homeschooled, we developed confidence in what we were pursuing.

> After about a year of homeschooling and meeting more people who homeschooled, we developed confidence in what we were pursuing.

What do I say to the nosy neighbor?

Everyone has that one neighbor who just doesn't have enough to do. She's the one who runs to her window every time a siren sounds. We had ours, too, living across the street. You know the type. These people have to be the first to cut their grass, plant spring flowers, and paint the house when it needs it. Their yards are perfect. Their cars are always clean. They never forget to put out their garbage, which amounts to one bag for the week.

The week after we pulled our children from the public school, that nosy neighbor nonchalantly strolled over to our house, professing to look at our roses. She also casually remarked that she had noticed our children weren't getting on the school bus. This was our chance to inform her that she might see our children a lot more and why.

It turned out that this woman felt that the American schools were lacking strength. She commended us for undertaking such a dutiful project and admitted our children would certainly learn more. She then confessed that she had passed many a student through the system who couldn't read at a fifth grade level. She had been a high school English teacher for twenty-five years. The nosy neighbor might just surprise you with admiration for your decision to homeschool.

> If everyone could be taught one-on-one, imagine how educated this world would be.

Does homeschooling really work?

You bet it does. Wouldn't you excel with one-on-one training? Home education guarantees a much lower ratio of students to teacher. Most private schools average about fifteen to twenty-five students per teacher. During the average forty-five-minute class period, a teacher spends fifteen minutes filling out paperwork, fifteen minutes handling disciplinary problems, and only fifteen minutes teaching.

In the last ten years there have been several studies conducted on homeschooling methods, social concerns, and general knowledge. Some of the independent studies have even been conducted by public schools. They show that homeschoolers score, on the average, thirty to forty percentile points higher on standardized achievement tests than students of public schools, which makes sense because of the one-on-one teaching. This does not mean that all homeschoolers are scoring high. All schools, whether they are public, private, or homeschools, have their failures. It takes a dedicated family to make homeschooling effective.

> Never feel guilty for not homeschooling all of your children. Some children need the competition that public and private schools provide.

Can I homeschool one of my children and send the other to a public or private school?

Yes, it is done quite often. Some children respond better to homeschooling than others, just as some children need the daily social interaction between students and teachers in public or private schools. Never feel guilty for not homeschooling all of your children. You are providing the best for each of your children. Each child is different in personality and in the way she learns.

In Summary

We bet you've possessed self-confidence all along and knew you were the most qualified person to educate your child. You've also learned why other families homeschool, which has made you less alone in this endeavor. By homeschooling, you know your children will have everything to gain in their educational and social well-being.

Perhaps you've considered an umbrella school to help you with the record keeping. You've also been pointed in the right direction about which states require mandatory testing, and you have a fair assessment of the positives and negatives of home-schooling. You aren't going to worry if the daily chores are being done. And you'll have to work on not letting yourself get over-whelmed. But, gee, there's so much more on your mind. So, quick, you better move on to the next chapter. It's sure to shed more light on the subject of homeschooling.

CHAPTER 3

Mothers, Careers, Guilt, and Homeschooling

Homeschooling on Your Mind, Mom?

Making the decision to homeschool is a huge responsibility for a parent to consider, but it's an even bigger one for the mother if she's going to be the primary teacher. That's because it often involves a career change decision on the mother's part. Please read this chapter with an open mind, and educate yourself to the possibilities available today. Homeschoolers come from many walks of life.

How many battles have you fought with your child over doing homework?

Dear Mom, We Need You to Wear One More Hat

You see that your child isn't doing well in school, perhaps even failing. Or maybe your gifted and talented child is losing interest in learning, becoming bored, or not feeling challenged at school. You've attended several parent/teacher conferences, taking time away from the job needed to support your family.

Your child complains his teacher doesn't like him. And your child's teacher, you found to your surprise, truly doesn't like your child. There is a huge personality clash, and the school administration isn't cooperating with your efforts to fix the problem. You don't like the teacher who is supposed to be educating your child, and now you are losing respect for the administration. What is a parent to do?

Children watch our actions more than they listen to our words.

The school stress is getting to your family. You don't understand where your tax dollars are being spent if the brand-new school your child attends doesn't have enough textbooks. Your child is in a classroom with forty students to one teacher, and the teacher is always a substitute on Fridays. Add all of the above to the normal stress of raising a family, and that puts your view of education at an all-time low.

We've all experienced situations of student/teacher personality clashes, but when it affects your child's education you have to do something about it as soon as possible. But you have that report due on Tuesday, a marketing meeting on Thursday, and groceries to get before going home tonight.

Out of sheer desperation and stress you tell your child, "You won't always get along with everyone, even teachers. Just do your best." You don't have time to deal with another problem that may go away in a few weeks. You know how kids can be. Besides, you're still in your suit and high heels cooking dinner at 8:00 at night, and your son needs help with his seemingly endless homework.

Don't the schools realize parents are working harder than ever? Don't they realize how tired everyone is at night? Is all this homework and added stress on your child that seems to be overflowing onto Mom's shoulders going to ease up a bit? Shouldn't the schools be teaching your child? Hold on for a moment.

Bashing the Current School Systems

Let's not bash the school systems of America. We can't fix the schools overnight, next month, or even a year from now. We can, in fact, fix the problem with how to educate your child.

Here's how homeschoolers look at the situation. We are the parents. As parents, it is our job that our children receive the best education we can give them. If the public school system is not meeting our expectation of a wonderful education, then we better find another alternative that does. If you want something done right, do it yourself. But at what cost to the mother? You are wondering if you will be able to wear one more hat.

A Loan for the Home Addition

How are you envisioning homeschooling your child? Are you picturing a classroom addition built onto the house that is already costing you too much to maintain? Have you ordered desks, chairs, teacher's cabinets, and a chalkboard for you to stand near with your pointer? Don't try to create the school your child is attending in the home environment. None of those items you imagine are as important as sitting on the couch beside your child reading together in a peaceful and no-stress situation. Besides, having a chalkboard isn't going to make your child learn her multiplication tables, which she should have mastered years ago.

> **Think of a classroom that consists of a couch and a coffee table. Now picture you and your child learning together in that environment.**

Has your pulse increased thinking that the solution must be found by you? Are you worried you'll have to quit your job to homeschool? Let's answer a few questions moms have asked us over the years.

Mom, Did You Wash My Favorite Jeans?

I feel so guilty thinking I should homeschool, but it'll be one more job for me to handle, and it makes me angry at the public school system as it exists today. What do I do?

We applaud the honest woman who can say that one more job, such as educating her child, would put her on overload. We'd rather have her admit that up front than halfway through her child's seventh grade year. There's nothing wrong with being honest, especially with yourself.

As for being angry at the public school system, lots of people are, even the teachers who have to teach in the system. There are books, magazines, newspapers, talk shows, and politicians discussing the school systems everywhere we turn. Yes, we've got problems, but there will never be a quick fix, so let go of the anger.

Why do I feel that I'm reteaching my child's homework each night?

Simply put, because you are. We got to a point where we believed our children when they said, "The teacher didn't go over this yet, so will you?" Children do have an unusual amount of homework today. Public school teachers confess that they can't accomplish all the work required of them because of the discipline problems interrupting precious class time. There's no point in placing blame on the schools, teachers, administration, parents, or students because there are many factors contributing to the problem.

I think homeschooling full-time would be financially impossible for our family. What can I do?

You're in control of your finances and know best if you could exist on less income. Take stock of how you live. If you pay for day care, school and business lunches, work and school clothing, and gas to and from work, you may find your paycheck isn't

SHANNA BASTIAN

"Before homeschooling I was frustrated, shy, and depressed all the time," says Shanna Bastian. "I had no confidence because no matter how hard I worked, I just couldn't seem to get it. I found only benefits in homeschooling. Without it, I would have fallen through the cracks of the system and been labeled learning disabled forever. Homeschooling allowed me to progress at my own pace and to pursue those things that I most needed at the time. I was able to grow in areas that would have never been addressed in the system. It gave me the opportunity to pursue my first love, art. I have participated in numerous art competitions and have received honors on the local and state levels. Our family grew so close and developed a love for one another that will last forever."

Shanna had struggled in the public school system from kindergarten to when she failed every subject in the fifth grade. Her parents had her independently tested and discovered that she couldn't even read three-letter words and only recognized the letters of the alphabet 8 percent of the time. Her parents immediately withdrew her and her two younger sisters and began the homeschooling process. Five months later, Shanna was reading on grade level, using Scriptures as her reading primer.

Shanna goes on to acknowledge, "My wonderful mother gave up her career as a broadcast journalist to homeschool me. She loved her career, and I realized that if she was willing to give that up for me, then I must be worth the effort." Now married and the mother of two little girls of her own, Shanna recently graduated and passed her state boards to pursue a nursing career. Shanna and her family have built their own home and are developing their dairy farm. She says, "My husband and I have already decided that we will homeschool our children. It is the only way to go!"

stretching as far as you think. Maybe one of you, mother or father, could stay at home to homeschool, if that's truly what you want to do. We already have shown you how homeschooling can be relatively inexpensive.

How will I know if I should homeschool?

Maybe it will be an academic decision to homeschool. Maybe it will be a safety necessity for your child. And maybe homeschooling will never be an option for your family. If you're waiting for somebody to tell you that you need to do it, that's the wrong way to begin homeschooling.

Your most important asset is your child.

Quite frankly, the homeschooling community scares me. They make me feel inadequate if I don't homeschool my child. Will I fit in with other homeschoolers?

The homeschooling community scares quite a few people. We go against the system by creating our own system.

Not all of us have wonderful and perfect children that we get along with every day. Raising children is a tough job, whether we homeschool or not. We homeschool our children for a vast amount of reasons: educational, spiritual, moral, safety, lifestyle, and so on. We have strong opinions about what has worked and not worked for us. Homeschooling is our way of saying the current system is not working for us. We don't have the time and energy to fix the system, so we must assist our children another way.

Homeschooling parents must be willing to accept full responsibility for their children's education.

But believe it or not, we're just as scared as you are of what is happening with America's educational system. We know it needs reform. We understand how hard the job is for teachers, principals, and administrators. Our hats are off to them for what they face every day. Imagine what the dedicated teacher must go through every day with the system the way it is.

However, we are being authoritative when we say that our children aren't going to go through the system by sliding in and out of the cracks. So, we become strong willed, speak our opinions, and take full responsibility for guiding our own children. And, yes, sometimes homeschooling parents become judgmental. We judge the schools, the system, the curriculum, the morals, and we shouldn't. When we make the conscious decision not to make those judgments, we discover homeschooling to its fullest.

Hiring Another Mom to Homeschool Your Child

Did you say I could hire another person to homeschool my child?

This may solve all your problems and the other mom's, too. You want to provide a better education for your child than what she is currently getting. You can't quit your job—and neither can your husband—to devote the time necessary for homeschooling. There is another homeschooling mom who has decided to quit her job or work part-time so she can homeschool her child, only it will be tough with less money coming into the house. If it can be arranged to your mutual satisfaction, pay her to teach your child. Problem solved—maybe.

You must live in a state that allows homeschooling to be done by someone other than the child's parent. Although no state can tell you not to hire a tutor for your child, it's best to understand your state's laws on what constitutes a tutor and what constitutes the homeschooling instructor. Your state may ask that you list who will be homeschooling your child along with the curriculum being used.

So, do your homework. By calling one of the state organizations listed at the back of this book and asking where you can obtain your state's rules and regulations about homeschooling, you'll have taken the first step to eliminating some of the stress in your life and your child's life.

Where do I find the homeschooling mom who would teach my child?

Well, she's probably in the Yellow Pages of your phone book, but you'd be there awhile trying to find her. You have to contact a support group in your area if you aren't in touch with the homeschooling community. Your support group will know about parents who want to teach other children. It's not as hard as you think to locate another homeschooler. She just might not live close to you. You'll have to think of it as driving your child to private school each day.

KEN AND ANN THOMPSON

Clover Academy, founded by Ken and Ann Thompson, functions as an alternative to traditional public education by providing supplemental instruction and/or guidance for the gifted student. The school uses the program developed by Northwestern University's Talent Search to guide the high school education of its students who want to shorten their high school commitment or enhance their high school curriculum. Thus far, the Thompsons have worked with six students, five currently in college and one entering next year. They credit their unique school to their having homeschooled their children. "Our only intent at first was to get our son out of the public school. Our daughter started taking classes at the community college in the seventh grade; our son, in the third grade. The gifted program in the public school was lacking what our children needed."

Ken and Ann like to refer to their students as hybrids because they have used almost every conceivable avenue to achieve the best education possible. They certainly have plenty to be proud of,

MOTHERS, CAREERS, GUILT, AND HOMESCHOOLING   71

A Word of Caution

Use caution when hiring other people to homeschool your child. You must keep tabs on what your child is learning. It is essential, and worth repeating, that the person homeschooling your child makes sure that your child is mastering each skill before moving on to the next lesson.

Interview a homeschooling tutor just as you would a day-care provider, a private school, or even a baby-sitter.

If you have a good relationship with the other homeschooling parent, there will be no problem.

Just as you would interview a day-care provider, a private school, or a baby-sitter, you must interview the parent who will be homeschooling your child. Ask yourself if you possess the same

with one student receiving a 35 on the ACT, and another taking her senior year at Indiana University while working for a physics profes-. sor and having a paper published before she entered college. All but one of their students have received scholarships based on need. One received a grant based on merit. Three were National Merit scholars, and one was a Bausch and Lomb winner.

"We have tutored four college sophomores; one at Carnegie Mellon University, one at the Honors College at the University of Michigan, another at the College of Business at Washington University, and the other at the University of Texas. We have a college freshman at Cornell College and two high school seniors that will go to Western Michigan in nursing and the University of Chicago."

Ken and Ann are working hard to enrich their students' education through supplemental tutoring. From their homeschooling experience, they emphasize that prospective homeschooling parents should seek out programs all over the country, not just locally, that provide the best possible education for their children. Clover Academy, which is registered with the Michigan Department of Education, is at P.O. Box 30008, Lansing, MI 48909. You may contact Ken and Ann Thompson via e-mail: drmom3@aol.com.

educational standards. No two families raise their children the same, but you will find families who have ideas similar to yours. That's what you're seeking in the shared homeschooling idea.

Homeschooling Grandparents

Don't forget about Grandma and Grandpa. If they are retired and want some company, what better company than their grandchildren? Grandparents make excellent teachers for your children. If a grandparent expresses a desire to help with the homeschooling process, whether it is part-time or full-time, accept his help.

How much should I pay another mom to homeschool my child?

Ask yourself, what is your child's education worth? Are you willing to pay a monthly fee comparable to private school tuition in your area? What were you paying in after-school day care? Should you add that fee onto the education fee if your child is going to stay with the tutor until you pick her up? Talk with the parent who will be doing the homeschooling and be honest and fair. Maybe the other mom doesn't require a huge amount of money for homeschooling your child. Instead, she needs a baby-sitter on the weekend, or someone to mow her lawn. We have friends who hire another parent to homeschool their two sons. They worked out a deal to pay the homeschooling parent's utility bills each month. In Texas, which gets hot and humid, our utility bills can be quite high.

It'll be the other parent's responsibility to make sure your child is truly learning each lesson before moving on. It'll be your responsibility to provide the curriculum, supplies, and your child's meals or other necessary things. You'll be able to take a look at your child's progress on a daily basis. The good news is there shouldn't be any reason for homework. Your evenings will be less stressful.

Foundation Skills

What are the foundation skills you mention throughout the book that my child should have?

Phonics, reading, comprehension, language, spelling, and basic math development are a good start. Our sons had no phonic knowledge, read but didn't understand what they read, and couldn't remember all their multiplication tables and some addition facts. We had to clean up the garbage first, before introducing new concepts.

We truly thought we were paying close attention to what they had been learning during their elementary years. We looked at every paper they brought home from the public school. We went to every school function. We read to them every night. We did flash cards on the weekends. We played educational board games. We just never had them read aloud to us. Have your children do this as much as possible. It reveals the gaps in their foundational skills.

Could I work part-time and homeschool?

Yes, yes, yes! Where there is the desire to help your child, there will be success. Many of us work part-time for the added income or time away from the family.

We Now Pronounce You Homeschooling Husband and Wife

My husband isn't sold on the idea of homeschooling, but I want to do it. What should I do?

This is a decision that must be made by both parents, for you'll need your husband's support if you're going to be doing most of the teaching. As parents, we like nice, simple patterns of family life. Get up, drop the kids off at school, go to work, come home, have dinner, live for the weekend. It gets old, but it's a pattern. Thinking about changing that pattern with homeschooling, a subject your husband might not know much about, may be what's upsetting him, not the actual homeschooling.

Many fathers have concerns about homeschooling that need to be addressed. To start off, ask him to read this book. Next, if your husband is a statistics person, get the facts about test results from HSLDA for him. More important, though, take him to a homeschooling support group meeting and encourage him to ask questions. We have listed concerns from fathers we have met. Possibly your husband has expressed one of these:

What athletic opportunities will be available?

My teen will never have a date.

Will my child be accepted by the college of her choice?

My child won't have any friends.

Will our child let us teach him?

I have to work fourteen-hour days; I can't teach him.

Will one of us have to quit our jobs?

Can we afford homeschooling?

Will my child have a high school diploma?

Will my son be able to get a job after high school?

Will we need to join some religious group?

Focus on your child's needs. Does your husband know that your child can't read at her current grade level? Plan to spend time calmly answering every question your husband has. You'll be armed with a wealth of homeschooling information to make your point.

Honey, Kids Will Be Kids

My husband seems to think I'm overreacting in the disappointment I feel about our child's educational level. What do I do?

Have you been carrying the full responsibility of keeping tabs on your child's education? If so, it's time to involve your husband more with the school your child is attending, your child's homework, parent-teacher conferences, and any other school situation. Show your husband your child's test grades, worksheets, and so on. Homeschooling isn't

> **Your children must feel they're worth your time.**

a decision to be made lightly. Make your disappointments about your child's school known and show your husband how homeschooling will improve your child's education.

How do I talk to my failing teenager about considering homeschooling?

Most parents who have had to begin homeschooling in their children's teenage years, including us, found our teens to be responsive to the idea. Teenagers know when they're in need of help. They may not be able to voice that they need your help, but that doesn't mean they don't want it. You must convey the message that you understand how they feel about making this change.

For those teens who resist the idea of homeschooling, you might approach the subject on a part-time or "try it for one year" basis. If your teens realize that you're willing to work with them for a solid year toward the goal of improving their academic skills, and know they can reenter the school system the following year with higher academics, their social concerns will be alleviated. One year might be all that's needed to set a teenager back on track. Invest in the time now, and the returns are guaranteed to be great.

Homeschooling Within the Public School System

Can I homeschool part-time and still send my child to public school?

What you are referring to is tutoring your children at home, so they can excel in the public school system. Let's look at both

JINEEN FERREIRA

Jineen Ferreira is a freshman in college majoring in early childhood education. She carries a 4.0 grade point average and was offered a full academic scholarship. When she graduates, she plans on teaching preschool or kindergarten age children.

Jineen began homeschooling in the sixth grade, and she recalls, "As a young teenager, I really hated the idea of being homeschooled at first and thought that I was going to die. However, I soon found out that there were many other homeschooled kids in my area, that I had plenty of friends. I went on several field trips with our support group, anything from skating to a teen club meeting. The general public loves saying that we homeschoolers aren't socialized, but that simply is false. The activities are out there. You just have to be willing to look for them."

Jineen points out that almost every life event can be educational. She and her family loved going to the park in the middle of the day, or taking a trip to the ocean to study science. She also studied German with help from another homeschooling mom. Jineen was very glad she had been given the opportunity to homeschool through her high school years. Before attending college, she wondered if she would be at the same level as her peers. Not only did she feel prepared beyond the average freshman level in college, she knew it was due to her mom's dedicated teaching methods. Jineen says adamantly, "Any mom who thinks that her children should try homeschooling should go for it. The experience for both the child and the parent is invaluable. I thank my mother and father for homeschooling me."

sides of this scenario. Part-time homeschooling works just fine if—and the if is big—some key factors are in place.

First, it won't be beneficial to homeschool part-time if it was safety reasons that led you to consider homeschooling in the first place. Other adjustments would need to be made to fix that type of situation.

Second, your child may be very tired at the end of the day and grow to resent the added hour or two you teach at home. However, being tired at the end of the school day could be from other causes, such as improper eating habits, not getting to bed early enough, poor eyesight or listening skills, or very low academic foundation skills.

Third, your curriculum may contradict the public school's curriculum. This can become a major concern. You would need to use the same books as the public school or choose a similar curriculum. You want to help your child with her education, not argue and confuse the situation.

Fourth, your child may experience burnout from education overload. You would need to decide what skills your child needs help with, and be careful to work on small tasks.

Last, and most important, you must be careful not to bad-mouth what he is learning in the public school in comparison to what is being taught at home. This will thoroughly confuse your child. If you're going to spend your time complaining or judging what and how your child is learning, well then, you better home-school full-time.

Homeschooling Part-Time: Benefits for the Child

Let's talk about homeschooling your child in a "part-time" manner while working within the public or private school system. We feel that if done right, this presents endless opportunities for your child. We're in the process of doing this with our youngest son, and we can attest that it works extremely well.

Homeschooling your child on key subjects such as language mechanics, writing, reading, and mathematics skills will definitely lead to her being placed in the honors or gifted and talented classes. The children in those classes didn't get there by themselves. They had mothers and fathers who read to them and taught them to love learning at a very young age. Whether those parents realize it or not, they were homeschooling their little ones before they even began school. Homeschooling your child for academic growth will place your child in those advanced classes.

Your child will be given opportunities to join social activities not as readily available to the homeschooler, such as working on the school newspaper and joining the speech and debate team, theater productions, chess club, foreign language clubs, fine art classes, and many others. Homeschooling is wonderful, and it affords many opportunities, but it has a long way to go to offer social activities of the public school caliber.

The sports opportunities will be unlimited. Homeschooling does offer team sports for both male and female students, but not at the competitive level of most public schools. Face it, the public schools have the sports, the gyms, the tracks and fields, the equipment, and the coaches for boys and girls. These things are important to middle and high school students.

By homeschooling part-time, your child will be able to participate in extracurricular activities and maintain a high grade point average—no sweat! He won't have to sit on the bench during high school games simply because he's not passing. The "no pass, no play" rule is being enforced.

Your child will be able to apply for academic scholarships with the help of the public school counselors. This is a concern for many students who want to go to college.

Your child will be able to juggle school, extracurricular activities, and a social life with ease. If the academic skills are in place, school becomes a breeze for the homeschooled high schooler.

Your child will be able to read assigned material with ease and comprehension. Reading is the key to all subjects, the key to success.

Homeschooling Part-Time: Benefits for the Parent

We can't discuss the benefits of part-time homeschooling for the child without listing the benefits afforded to the parents. The obvious benefit to the parent is, of course, that it's less time consuming, and that's something all of us are concerned with, especially if you continue to work full-time.

You won't be responsible for keeping your child's records, credits in high school, transcripts, or test results. That doesn't mean you shouldn't pay attention to all of the above, checking for accuracy in the reporting being done by your child's school. This is very important. Many school records are inaccurate.

You'll have less frustration in helping your child with homework and school projects.

You'll decide when and for how many hours you'll homeschool. We found just an hour or two on a weekend was enough to keep our son ahead of his course level. We made sure we were always teaching him the next lesson in his math course, so when the lesson was explained during class, it was a review for him.

There will be less stress in making sure your child joins social activities, and—the factor we enjoy—you won't have to drive so far to get to those activities.

Homeschooling for a Year or Two

If I decide to homeschool for a year or two to work on my child's academic skills, in what school years should I do this?

You must ask yourself, where are my child's skills right now? Is he doing fine in the public school, right on target, above average, or below average? Homeschooling through the elementary years sets the foundation skills into place. Homeschooling in the middle school years continues that process or cleans up the skills if they weren't achieved in public elementary school.

If we had to do it again, we would have homeschooled first through sixth grade, then entered our children in the public or private schools in their seventh through twelfth grades. Their skills, by that time, would have been above average, and they would be ready for the social interaction, sports, clubs, and so forth that middle school and high school afford.

Don't plan on homeschooling your high schooler in ninth or tenth grade, then placing her back in the public school for eleventh and twelfth grades. We say, "Don't mess with the high school years!" The public schools are going to suggest and possibly insist that your child test for credit validity in each course.

The Above-Average Child

Should I homeschool my child if he is gifted and talented?

Gifted and talented children don't need more homework.

If your child is gifted and talented (and yes, we realize that is a public school term), but the school he is attending doesn't have a program advanced enough to meet his needs, you'll have to address this problem. Homeschooling may or may not be the answer for you. There are plenty of advanced-level courses in the curricula on the market. We don't believe, however, that you can tailor any course to become an advanced course just by giving your child more work to do. Gifted and talented students need different perspectives on how to view a course, not more homework.

If you have a gifted and talented child, evaluate whether she needs that competitive edge that only a classroom can give. Homeschooling alone with you may make your child feel less productive. This is not what you're trying to achieve by homeschooling.

Perhaps you could look into a private school that offers a core concentrated advanced program. Or, depending on the age of your child, supplement courses given by tutors or college professors or by correspondence would keep your child's interest level high. Don't rule out homeschooling; just prepare yourself for a challenging project.

Contact the Utgnet (Uniqueness, Twice-Gifted & Gifted Network) organization for information at its e-mail address: Uni Gift@aol.com.

Iowa Test, Stanford Achievement Test

Even though I may decide to keep my child in the public school system, should I have him tested yearly outside the system?

Despite the fact that the schools conduct tests themselves, many homeschooling families don't trust the public school tests to be complete evaluations. Remember that our eighth grade son, in a public school, only read at a fifth grade level after we had him tested. Had we relied on the school test, we never would have realized his reading deficiency. You decide what you want to test for your child.

Contact Bob Jones University for a list of testing options and certified testers in your area: 1-800-845-5731 or http://www. bju.edu.

Tutors Needed

What are the first signs that my child's skills are weak?

Very good question! We have listed a few, but don't limit yourself just to these clues.

Pay attention to elementary children who say they have a bellyache or headache more than once or twice a month before leaving for school.

Listen to what your child has to say about her teachers and classes. Elementary children should learn with enthusiasm. If it's not there, something is wrong.

Ask your children to read aloud to you from their textbooks, readers, and worksheets sent home. Do this often. Chances are their reading skills are low if they complain about having to read aloud. Listen to how they sound out words, then ask them to tell you what they read. Are they comprehending?

Make sure they're bringing work home. A sure sign of failing grades is when your child doesn't ever show you any work.

> You, and only you, are the one constant factor in your child's life.

Know your child's friends. If the friends are good students, chances are your child is a good student.

Have your children measure things around the house. Can they read a ruler?

See if they can tell time using a clock with a face, not a digital clock.

Play educational games with them, and note if they complain about playing the game.

If the school nurse calls you several times to say your child isn't feeling well but has no fever or significant signs of illness, you might ask his teacher what she was teaching at the time he needed to go to the nurse. The skills are introduced in the elementary school years, so keep your eyes and ears open.

Is your child causing trouble or perhaps becoming the class clown? These can be warning signs at any age.

Do tutoring facilities help with a child's foundation skills?

Call a tutoring center near you and make an appointment to talk with staff. Leaving your child in a public school but having him tutored professionally might be all that is needed to improve his academic skills. Just make sure to discuss with the facility's representatives the need for improving the fundamentals and how you can help with the process. Tutoring centers can be expensive, but can also provide excellent results.

Can I hire a homeschooling parent to be a tutor to my public school child?

We tutor public school children each summer. Having their friends join us was a way to get our children to keep homeschooling the essentials like reading, math facts, and language mechanics. It got to be that a parent would ask one of us to tutor his child in a particular weak area of course work. It seemed that most students we've tutored needed help in language mechanics, basic math skills with fraction work, and writing. We were happy to do it, so ask a homeschooling parent if she would be willing to tutor your child.

Help, I Need to Get Out of the House Once in Awhile

Is there a homeschooling mothers' group I can join?

Ask your local homeschooling support group that question. We had a homeschooling moms' group that got together twice a month for dinner and a movie out, away from the kids! The moms even made a pact that there would be no talking about homeschooling or the children for the entire evening. We could talk about crafts, books, movies, trends, and recipes, but not homeschooling.

My kids drive me nuts and, at times, going to work seems easier. What do I do?

All kids drive their parents nuts at some time or another. If they didn't, they wouldn't be normal. And, we have to agree with you, going to work does seem easier, especially having lunch out each day. However, we're talking about your child's education. You have some choices to make. This is why you must feel absolutely certain that you want to homeschool your child. Don't start homeschooling if you resent having to give up certain wants. Don't homeschool if you know you don't want to do so. But don't not homeschool simply because you think your child will drive you crazy.

Homeschooling is very different from the mass education taking place in this country. In an unhurried atmosphere that promotes a stress-free environment, a child can't help but learn and retain. Your child won't drive you crazy if you both aren't running on high stress levels.

I'm not an organized person. How will I be able to homeschool?

You'll need to set goals that focus and prioritize the day so that the bulk of your energy will be directed to accomplishing the objectives that are the key to achieving the educational purpose of homeschooling. Sounds like what your manager at work dictates? Ignore it.

The reason you feel disorganized is because you're being Supermom at work, at home, and with your children. Homeschooling is going to change you and the way your family views life. Don't worry about being organized. Just sit beside your child and teach her to read. Reading takes place even if the laundry isn't folded, the ironing board is set up in the family room, the checkbook needs balancing, and the dog needs a bath.

Mama's Boy

Is it healthy for a child to spend so much time with his parent, let alone his parent/teacher?

Wow, that is a tough question to answer. Do the parent and the child have an excellent relationship? We've met people who have claimed that homeschoolers tend to be led around by their parents on a leash, so to speak. We've heard the remark "mama's boy." We also have an idea of what those people who challenge the homeschooling methods are trying to express. They seem to be concerned that homeschoolers are segregated from their peers, thus they rely on their parents' values more than developing their own. Well, we think a general evaluation of all homeschoolers is unwarranted, but above that, we would rather have our children rely on our values than values set by peer pressure while they're developing their conception of what is right and wrong.

Peer pressure can destroy the motivation to learn. Has your child been afraid to answer a question in class for fear of being laughed at by his peers?

Perhaps homeschoolers are viewed as shy or quiet by those who are unaware of what homeschooling actually involves. However, most homeschooling families have taught their children to speak intelligently and politely. If a homeschooler doesn't appear to be boisterous in a crowd, it might not be from shyness. He may be surveying the surroundings with an adultlike perception. The more educated a child becomes, the more likely he is to rationalize situations from all perspectives. Thus, he is taught "Think before you act."

Talk to a homeschooler, or better yet, have the child you're considering homeschooling talk to another homeschooler. You'll be surprised how well a homeschooled child can carry on a conversation with a person of any age. When you homeschool your children, you'll begin to see them open up and ask questions. They won't be afraid of failure, because they'll know if they try, they won't fail.

Your expectations will either limit or unleash your child's potential.

Am I being overly cautious about my child's education by wanting to homeschool?

Maybe. Even if you are, so what? As parents we want the best we can afford for our children: the best living conditions, the best food in their stomachs, the best safety concerns, and the best educational standards. If we are overly cautious about their education, so be it. This world is tough. They'll need to get a job to support themselves and a family someday. Let's equip our children with the tools necessary to achieve those goals.

How many years will I need to homeschool?

You'll need to homeschool for as long as your child needs an education. If you're homeschooling to bring your child's academic level up so she can reenter the public school, you'll know when that has happened. If you're homeschooling for safety purposes, you'll continue to do so until your situation is better. If you're homeschooling because you feel you're the best person available to educate your child, well, we guess you're in it for the long haul.

In Summary

Mom, this chapter was for you, and we hope it answered those difficult questions. You are your children's greatest asset. You understand their every need. You know when they fail, and you know you can help them to succeed. This chapter has given you some available options. Remember, there are no quick fixes. Homeschooling takes valuable time.

Keep reading and researching how homeschooling might benefit your situation. Learn your state's homeschooling laws to see if you can hire someone to assist you, or consider a tutor. Certainly give some thought to part-time homeschooling. Always remember that you'll make the ultimate decision on whether homeschooling is for your family or not. Now, let's continue by giving you the specifics about curricula and how to choose an appropriate one for your child.

CHAPTER 4

Curricula and How to Choose the Best One

Which Curriculum Is Best?

Nobody can tell you which curriculum is best for your child. Other homeschoolers can guide you, give their opinions, or even recommend, but only you will know which curriculum will best suit your child's needs. Incidentally, you will change that curriculum at least once as time progresses.

> Everyone will have an opinion about which curriculum is the best. Only your opinion will count.

We never chose just one curriculum for all the subjects, but we had our favorites. For instance, we loved *Glencoe Essential Mathematics for Life* for its task-oriented design, but we didn't use that curriculum in other subjects. We chose courses from a variety of curriculum providers, and we admit to being enticed by the packaging and professions of what each course could provide our children. Some worked, some didn't.

How to Choose Wisely

You may choose a broad-based English curriculum that moves quickly for your son who doesn't enjoy language mechanics and literature, and a detailed English curriculum for your daughter who wants to read literature by famous female authors. Or how about Algebra I for the ten-year-old who's a whiz at mathematics? This will be left to your discretion. Just don't be too hard on yourself for choosing one that simply doesn't fit your needs. We've all done it. In the end, it's the quality of teaching that counts, not the curriculum.

You'll soon be attending curriculum seminars and become an old pro at selecting the textbooks that best suit your child's needs. We enjoyed going to the homeschooling book sales to see what was new each year. Our children would roll their eyes at us as we prepared for one of those book sales. They knew we would be home with another new course to try.

In the meantime, we're going to flood you with options available in textbooks, videos, and software throughout the book. Call a few, call them all, but at least call the ones that look interesting. You'll soon have a mailbox full of homeschooling options.

Where to Begin

How will I know what types of curricula are available?

You'll have to call and request brochures from the curriculum providers. Are you looking for a visual textbook with colorful photos accompanied by videos? How about task-oriented booklets that can be finished every few weeks instead of one large textbook? Maybe you'll choose software accompanied by a workbook. What about manipulatives, games, or experiments done with an accompanying handbook? Straight reading text for the advanced reader might be what you need. Repetitive booklets to reinforce fundamentals could be the way to go. Well, get on the phone, surf the Web sites we've given you, or write for information.

How will I know at what level to begin?

Good question! You could pick up the book *How Do You Know They Know What They Know?* from Grove Publishing. It's an excellent resource to evaluate your child's progress and to answer the questions "What does my child already know?" and "What does she need to learn next?"

If you have a child ready to begin the first grade, then you can order your first grade curriculum and move along at your child's pace. If, however, you're pulling your child out of elementary, middle, or possibly high school, you might want to have him tested.

How Do You Test Your Own Child?

We found the true test for our children was not to give them an academic knowledge test, but rather to hand them a book supposedly written for their level and ask them to read aloud to us for about thirty minutes. Oh my, does reading aloud reveal wonders.

It took every bit of our effort to hold back a horrified grimace. Hey, it took biting the sides of our mouths not to let the unwarranted remarks escape.

> **Having your child read aloud will reveal wonders.**

Ultimately, it took every bit of our patience to sit quietly and listen. And listen we did for thirty minutes that felt like thirty hours, glancing at each other in disbelief. All this time, we thought we had been paying attention to our sons' education. We'd attended PTO meetings, helped with homework and major grade projects, looked through their work and textbooks, but we had never even considered asking them to read aloud. So we knew immediately where to begin. No academically scored test would have revealed so much. Actually, the school's testing set them above target when compared with other students across the country. We would have to start all over and teach the boys to read.

How to Discover Children's Reading Level

If you don't know whether a book is written at your child's current grade level, there are some simple ways to find out. Most children's books state on the cover or back jacket the age level for which the books are written. It might be something like this: Suggested level 4.5. The 4 stands for the fourth year or grade, and the 5 stands for the fifth school month in that grade. If the particular book you choose doesn't display the grade level, ask the bookstore to help. Better yet, go to the library and have the librarian assist you. Don't ask your child's public school teacher. There are too many students per class for even the most outstanding teacher to know your individual child's level.

Improving reading academics is an excellent reason to homeschool for at least a year.

When testing your child, select a book one level below and another one level above what your child's current grade is. Have your child read the book that is one level below first. You are looking for clarity, correct pronunciation of words, and correct sounding out procedures. We would say look for phonics capabilities, but not all students have been taught phonics.

After your child reads a few pages to you, ask him to tell you what he just read in his own words to check comprehension. If all goes well, hand him the book in the grade level just above his current grade and complete the same test. You'll have a good estimate of his reading level, and an estimate is all you need to get started.

Can't Believe What You Hear?

Remember to listen with a pleasant look on your face, which is hard to do when you realize your child can't sound out words in the sixth grade. Don't cause discouragement with comments not necessarily directed at them, such as, "I can't believe you never learned to sound out those words. What in the world have you been doing in school?" This test was a rude awakening for our family and one of the reasons we knew we needed to homeschool.

By the way, improving reading academics is an excellent reason to homeschool for at least a year.

Helpful Hint

Determine your child's reading level and begin all other courses in that grade level. If your child can't read well, it won't help her to be in a higher-level science or math subject when she first begins homeschooling. Note that textbook information, directions, and study questions are written per the course level. Reading at a third grade level in a sixth grade math course won't promote a success-ful result. The beginning process may need fine-tuning and cleanup of skills. As you continue working with your child, you'll be able to move faster.

Do I create a test for my child that determines grade level, or can I purchase one?

You can use the reading level test mentioned above to deter-mine grade level or purchase a scholastic achievement test from the curriculum provider Bob Jones University, 1-800-845-5731. It will supply information on all the types of tests it offers. It will also give you the name of a certified tester in your area. We recommend you ask your support group members who they use. There are plenty of ex-schoolteachers homeschooling their own children who would be happy to test your child for you. Bob Jones University offers a registration for degreed teachers to become certified testers for homeschoolers. Keep all test results in a file.

Some states require testing and provide this service annu-ally. We recommend you have your child tested simply to know where to begin, if you have a middle or high schooler whom you have decided to homeschool. If you have a pretty fair assessment of your child's level, simply start there.

How will I know what curriculum suits my child?

Even after you test your child, you may not know at first. This is a trial-and-error project at the beginning. Let's say you choose not to have your child tested before you begin, because you know at what grade level to begin. The next decision is to choose the books you'll use. Call each of the companies we have provided in the curriculum list and ask it to send you a catalogue. Or ask the members of your support group to let you look through their catalogues and textbooks. Some of the catalogues give detailed information about each textbook with photos of the chapter highlights. It may be that simple.

> **Choose a curriculum that appeals to your child. You can always change your mind down the road.**

Now, let's pretend it wasn't that easy. The catalogues were concise in description and certainly showed colorful photos, but you need more information. Most suppliers have toll-free numbers to call just for that purpose. They're happy to spend as much time as you need to describe their textbooks. We found each of the curriculum suppliers extremely helpful.

But I want to look through the curriculum before I purchase it. Can I do that?

And you should. You wouldn't purchase an automobile without a test-drive, so take a look at the curriculum before you purchase it. This is easy to do. Some of the curriculum suppliers tour cities displaying their textbooks. They're referred to as "curriculum fairs," "book fairs," "book tours," or "homeschooling conferences." When you place your calls to the curriculum publishers, ask for a list of displays in your area. As soon as your name is placed on several homeschooling mailing lists, you'll receive information on the fairs and conferences held in your area. In the meantime, take a look at other homeschoolers' textbooks.

Touchy Situations

What is a touchy situation?

Touchy situations are ones that left you no choice but to quickly pull your child from a public or private school. They're not situations in which your child was expelled from his public or private school. Now your child is at home and you need to educate him.

But what if time didn't permit the luxury of looking over several curricula? Your child was in a rough situation at public school and circumstances dictated you withdraw him immediately for the sake of his safety or health. This is where you must know your state's rules on necessary curricula. Some states require that the curriculum be in place before withdrawing your child. You can always begin with a temporary curriculum and change down the road.

Unsupervised Learning Is Not Homeschooling

Don't aggravate a terrible situation by not really educating your child when you withdraw him from school. We've met people who thought a child could learn sitting at a computer unsupervised, playing computer games and touring the Internet. This is not homeschooling. As a matter of fact, it's an embarrassment to the homeschool community to have families take advantage of the homeschooling laws only as a baby-sitter for their dropouts.

We live in a state where a homeschool is considered a private school, which made it easy. We created our own written curriculum until the textbooks arrived. There are plenty of copies of textbooks from the public schools at the library. You can't check out these books, but you can certainly create lessons from them until your textbooks arrive.

Homeschooling for Religious Purposes

Do I need to choose a Bible-based curriculum to homeschool?

You need to choose a curriculum that suits your child's needs. This is your main concern. It's left up to the parent to decide whether to incorporate religion into the curriculum. Your job is to teach the specific subjects required by your state. Any other subjects you teach are definitely your choice.

I want to homeschool my child for religious purposes. What is available for my child?

You'll have no problem finding a curriculum to meet your needs, for homeschooling was founded by some of the most spiritual families in America. Just a few years ago, it was actually easier to find a curriculum that was spiritually based. Some are heavily spiritual and some are what we classify as written with good morals. Contact Bob Jones University, 1-800-845-5731, or A Beka, 1-800-874-2352, and ask it to send you its catalogues. These curricula are excellent even for those who don't choose them for the religious factor. You'll choose the best curriculum for your child, making sure to review the material thoroughly. Join a spiritual support group or start your own at your church. There are plenty of homeschoolers who educate for religious purposes.

Specific Curricula

Can I tailor my child's curriculum to meet a specific need?

This is the whole idea behind homeschooling. Let's assume you have a daughter who dreams of becoming a scientist. Science would be her strongest subject. You might want to construct her language and writing courses to encompass science information. You can design science vocabulary and spelling words to complement her science textbook. For example, she could locate the adjective clauses in her book on the planets. And she could do book reports on famous women scientists.

When you discover a topic your children love, incorporate it into as many subjects as possible. We don't mean to suggest that a child who dreams of becoming a baseball player play ball in the backyard all day, but rather read about famous baseball players in his reading course.

JULIE PERSINGER

"I could spend part of an evening or weekend working on school if I needed to, and didn't feel the pressure of having to rush to meet a group deadline," says Julie. "I truly feel like homeschooling helped me rediscover the joy of learning. In public school, I was often told word-for-word what I would need to know for an exam. That certainly wasn't the case with the homeschool curriculum I used!"

Julie Persinger, from Tennessee, chose homeschooling in her high school years for its flexibility. She attended public and private schools before choosing to homeschool. Julie was studying to be a concert pianist, which often led to traveling great distances for lessons and performances.

Julie is a graduate of Wheaton College with a degree in piano performance. After college she lived in England for a year, working as a church volunteer. Now married and looking forward to homeschooling her children one day, Julie says, "If I could have had a choice, I would rather have been homeschooled all the way from kindergarten through high school. I am not quick to suggest homeschooling to many people because there are so many factors to consider, factors that many parents are not equipped or willing to deal with; however, I was a good candidate, which led to a successful homeschool experience. Homeschooling is not easy—it takes a lot of time, energy, and determination—but the rewards are wonderful!"

This is the best part about homeschooling. Incorporating lessons into your curriculum plan can be as exciting and fulfilling for the parent as it is for the child. We had a wonderful time preparing supplements on Egyptian history, medieval times, famous composers, and others.

No Textbooks

Can my child learn by asking me questions instead of using a textbook?

Your child will learn by asking you and others questions at any time, not just while homeschooling. Your question is whether or not your child will learn just from asking questions. If we all had the perfect child who thirsted for knowledge and knew what questions he wanted to ask, we could answer this with a confident "yes." But, we can't. Some "unschoolers" believe in question-provoked learning unaided by textbooks, and it works for many families. We're not unschoolers, but rather homeschoolers. We needed textbooks to provoke questions from our children.

I want my child to learn through exploring and talking with me. Don't textbooks squash creativity?

Your children will learn to explore and talk with you just because you're their parent and you care about them. If you believe textbooks squash creativity, we suggest that you read the books on unschooling theories. It's not fair of us to discuss the unschooling techniques when we're textbook-driven homeschoolers. There are many successful unschoolers who don't use textbooks. Ask your local bookstore to assist you with books on unschooling.

Do I have to use textbooks for every course my child studies?

Taking a nature walk, touring a zoo, or tending a garden is homeschooling as well.

No. You can use worksheets, supplements, videos, software, reading materials, magazines, and newspaper articles to teach just about any subject. They would be considered supplements to your child's particular curriculum. Supplements are wonderful to design for your own child. For our government studies we used the newspaper to its fullest every day. For geography studies we used blank maps and learned to label them until the children could do it in their sleep.

We did use textbooks as well as all the supplements named above. We found many excellent textbooks that we devoured cover to cover. For parents who don't feel they could constructively explain all the aspects of a particular course, textbooks are a reliable form of study.

I want to help my children with specific needs beyond their courses. How do I do this?

What you're referring to, we call a supplement. We discuss in detail how to prepare a written or activity supplement for your child in chapter 9. Here's a brief explanation of how to prepare a supplement: We simply checked out every book available on the subject, then read through the books, made notes, and developed activities, quizzes, and field trips to go with the course. You can decide how many weeks to spend on the supplement, how detailed the supplement becomes, and what subjects to cover.

> Spend as much time as your children need on a specific lesson for them to completely understand the concept.

What if I discover while teaching my child from the textbook that I need to spend more time on a specific need?

As you begin the homeschooling process, you'll find areas in which your child will need extra practice. The textbook may not provide enough practice for your child's particular weakness. Don't worry or assume the curriculum isn't thorough enough for your child's needs. Create supplemental worksheets as extra practice and take your time making sure your child retains the information needed to move on to the next lesson.

Honor Students

Is there an honors program for my child?

Yes. Some curricula offer higher-level courses. And you, of course, can design the courses for advanced levels as you see fit. Work at your child's pace, though. Pushing your child to attain honors or advanced course levels just for the sake of saying your child is advanced isn't what we're stressing. Teach for your child to learn, which might mean moving slower in the subjects that are harder for your child and faster in the courses in which your child thrives.

The Child with Special Needs

Curricula are available for children with special needs. Academic Therapy Publications specializes in curricula for learning disabled children and offers tests in most subjects. The curriculum mate-

JOHN NORDSTROM

"In homeschool I was allowed to work at my own pace to get back on track. I worked so hard, and I sometimes wanted to give up, especially on writing, but my mother kept after me about my potential and kept me going. I learned how to work hard, thanks to my mother. This work ethic has transferred into everything I do, from my schoolwork to each sport or activity in which I have participated, even to my student job here at college."

John Nordstrom is in college preparing for his engineering and physics degrees. This dedicated young man began homeschooling in the summer before fourth grade for the plain and simple reason that he could not read. In fact, he could not spell or recognize his own last name. John has dyslexia. While in the public school system he was called stupid, dumb, and retarded by teachers and students. With the help of John's dedicated parents and an eye specialist, whom he saw twice a week, he worked hard to overcome his learning disability while homeschooling from the fourth through the eighth grades.

rials are available from pre-K to secondary adult. Contact Academic Therapy Publications, Ann Arbor Publishers, High Noon Books, 20 Commercial Blvd., Novato, CA 94949, (415) 883-3314 or 1-800-422-7249.

In addition, we recommend that you get in touch with one of the organizations listed below. It will be more than happy to answer all your questions and recommend materials. Your child will advance just because homeschooling provides one-on-one training.

> National Handicapped Homeschoolers Association Network, 5383 Alpine Rd., SE, Olalla, WA 98359, e-mail: Nathanews@aol.com

> Hadley School for the Blind, P.O. Box 299, Winnetka, IL 60093, (847) 446-8111

When John reentered public school in his high school years, his academic abilities were stronger. In basketball he was the team captain, lettered three times, and won the "Most Improved" award and the "Coach's Award." In addition to excelling in basketball, he lettered in track and field twice, was the newspaper sports editor, a Quill and Scroll member, and won the Gold Medallion award for second place in state sports writing. He was the managing editor, assistant editor, student life writer, sports layout director, and reporter for the yearbook, as well as vice president of the National Honor Society, lettering in the Quiz Bowl and in academics.

John remembers, "One of the most meaningful activities I participated in during high school was helping at the elementary school. I spent time working one-on-one with poor readers. Being able to listen to them struggling through their lessons and encouraging them to hang in there, assuring them that they were smart and capable, even if they weren't great readers, was something that meant as much to me as it did to them."

John wants prospective homeschoolers to know that the most valuable lesson he learned from homeschooling is always to strive for your personal best. In John's case, he never let his dyslexia stand in the way of his dreams.

American Foundation for the Blind, 11 Pen Plaza, Suite 300, New York, NY 10001-2018, (212) 502-7600

National Association for the Deaf, 814 Thayer Ave., Silver Spring, MD 20910

Utgnet: Uniqueness, Twice-Gifted & Gifted Network, e-mail: UniGift@aol.com

Learning Disabilities Association of America, 4156 Library Rd., Pittsburgh, PA 15234, (412) 341-1515

CHADD (Children and Adults with ADD), 499 NW 70th Ave., Suite 308, Plantation, FL 33317, (305) 587-3700

What's the most important subject
I should teach my child?

Everyone will have a different choice. Our choice was reading. Just about all of our children's reading was done aloud. It was the only way we could tell if they were comprehending what they read, pronouncing words correctly, and focusing on the subject. Face it, every subject requires good reading skills. Why not give them excellent reading skills?

You may start off lucky with a child who is an avid reader, and therefore feel that learning math skills will be the most important. You're the best judge of what skills and subjects to study most. For that matter, you'll decide how much time to spend on each skill. If mathematics requires reinforcement in the multiplication area, then go for it. Spend the time, take the time, and use the time to teach.

Teacher's Editions

Will I need to purchase the teacher's edition for all
the textbooks?

It will depend on your knowledge of the course being taught. Some of the textbooks have the answers listed in the back of the book, and you won't need the teacher's edition. That will save on the expense. Ask your curriculum supplier for details about teacher's editions.

Possibly you can get through the elementary and middle school years with limited teacher's editions. Keep in mind, however, that some teacher's editions give unique "extra" things to do with each course.

Incorporating Computer Courses into Homeschooling

Can I teach my child with computer and video courses?

Absolutely. There are wonderful software courses just as good, if not better, than some textbook courses. Visit any computer store and see what is available. Browse through the wonderful catalogues for homeschooling and you'll be astonished, even enlightened, at what's available for your child.

Self-Taught Homeschoolers

We don't recommend all courses be taught using the computer. Part of the beauty of homeschooling is the interaction that takes place when working with your child. Don't let the computer become your child's teacher in every course. A parent should view the course right beside the child to make sure it's being used to its fullest potential. There are several programs available that, simply put, do nothing but flash colors and noises on the screen with little educational value.

Don't let the computer become your child's only teacher.

Do your research before purchasing a program. Teach your child everything there is to know about your particular computer. That's a computer course in itself. Computers are best used as a supplement to your child's education. Here are a few companies to get you started in your educational software research:

The Edutainment Catalog, 1-800-338-3844,
   http://www.edutainco.com

I.Q. Smart Education Software, 1-888-460-8923

You can also purchase comprehensive packages of software curricula at your local bookstore. Try some of these for your preview of software:

Alpha Omega Publications, 300 N. McKemy Ave., Chandler,
   AZ 85226-2618, (602) 438-2717, 1-800-622-3070,
   www.home-schooling.com. A Christian education
   software catalogue is available.

Bob Jones University Press, 1-800-845-5731. Christian
   philosophy educational computer programs for
   independent or directed use.

> There are plenty of software curricula that are pretty to look at, but not necessarily educationally sound. Ask for a software demonstration before purchasing.

Carolina Biological Supply Company, 2700 York Rd., Burlington, NC 27215-3398, (910) 584-0381, 1-800-334-5551, http:// www.carosci.com. A very large selection of science and math software.

Davidson & Associates, Inc., P.O. Box 2961, Torrance, CA 90509, 1-800-545-7677, http:// www.dvd.com. Educational software called *The Educational Advantage* for writing, language arts, reading, math, history, typing, science, ESL, and more.

Do I need to purchase a computer to homeschool?

It sure would make life easier. However, we use our computer for everything from balancing the checkbook to preparing transcripts. If you haven't used a computer, maybe it's time for you to take a course yourself. As a matter of fact, when you purchase your computer (and you'll want to get help from an experienced user on which type of system you should purchase), pick up a course in computer science that you and your child can learn together. Let your child lead the course. She'll pick up the computer jargon much faster than you will.

For those who don't believe in using computers, you can homeschool without a computer. You just will be missing a technological advancement in education.

Specific Course Selections: Phonics

Should I teach phonics?

Yes. No matter at what level you are beginning, the homeschooling process teaches phonics. It may seem childish to your sixth grader, but it will improve his reading and spelling skills.

> **Phonics flash cards are for all ages.**

When we first began, our children couldn't read fluently. They stumbled at words that were hyphenated at the end of the line. It meant nothing to tell them to sound out the word. They simply didn't know where to begin. Reading aloud revealed their phonics weakness on which we needed to work.

Emphasize Selected Courses

Your first job is to contact your state's homeschool organization to get a list of the required subjects for each grade level. Besides what is required by your state's guidelines, there are a variety of subjects that we felt were necessary. You may choose to follow some of our suggestions or create your own.

Research

Learning to research was important to us. We made sure our children visited the library twice a month. Teaching our children how to use the library's resources was done when they were very young. Research reports were assigned monthly, basically until our children could do them in their sleep. We gave them subjects they enjoyed to research. For a full year our youngest did basketball reports that consisted of enough statistics to make the head spin, but when the year was up, he was an expert in the field.

The librarian worked for her paycheck on the days our sons were there. If they couldn't find a book in the library's computer database, they had her searching. Our sons learned not to fear research, which led to them becoming better writers.

Writing

We also set aside twenty minutes per day for creative writing. Each child had a blank book purchased from a local bookstore (they come in several colors and fabrics) in which to write. They chose a topic out of a jar that contained several selections, such as: "What if you were the pilot of a major airline and an engine went out?" or "You are going camping in the wilderness. What will you need to bring?" We gave them twenty minutes for freestyle expression writing. Their essays were read aloud and discussed each day. It made for some interesting conversations.

We've been impressed with all the writing courses that are now being offered. Perhaps you would like to take advantage of some of these:

> AccuWrite, 4536 SW 14 Ave., Cape Coral, FL 33914,
> (941) 549-4400

> Bob Jones University, The Write Book Course,
> 1-800-845-5731

> National Writing Institute, 7946 Wright Rd., Niles, MI
> 49120, (616) 684-5375

> Zaner-Bloser, 2200 W. 5th Ave., P.O. Box 16764,
> Columbus, OH 43216-6764, 1-800-421-3018

Typing

Another suggestion is to teach your child how to type correctly, not the hunt-and-peck method. Only it isn't call "typing" any longer; it's "keyboarding." It's amazing how many children have fancy computers but use the one-finger method to type a report. We suggest you don't wait until their high school years to enter typing into their curriculum. They live in a computer world. They need to type. Select one of the many software typing courses available, such as:

> *Mavis Beacon Teaches Typing!* CD-ROM from Education Insights
>
> *Typing Tutor 7*, CD-ROM, from Simon & Schuster

Taking Notes

One of the things we noticed in the high school years is that we had neglected to teach our high schooler how to take notes. At the last minute, during his junior year, we showed him how to listen and take notes. He was going to take college courses in his senior year, and we assumed he'd know what was important to study. Not so. Homeschoolers tend to work at their own pace; thus, it is total culture shock when they are placed in a class where a professor lectures to a large mass of students. They try writing down everything the professor says. They even try learning everything that was covered in class before they know what will be expected of them when taking the exam. In other words, they tend to over-prepare, when all they need to do is relax and listen.

You may want to make cassette recordings of famous speeches or lectures. Have your child listen to the lecture and take notes. Then give him a quiz on what you think was important and worth remembering. Let him take the quiz with his notes. It will assess whether he is taking efficient notes. This should be done often to prepare your child for other teachers.

Counting Money

Another topic worth mentioning is counting money. How many times have you been at the store and been handed your change without having it counted back to you, only to discover it's the incorrect amount? In a generation that's obsessed with making lots of money, you'll find children who can't count back money when making change. This is worth spending time to learn.

For one month we gave our sons problems that required them to make change and count back the money aloud, using real money or Monopoly money. It worked wonders. Now, when our children go shopping they know how much money they should receive back in change before the cash register displays the amount. Our sons also notice how many cashiers need to wait for the register display before knowing the correct amount of change to give back to a customer, even when it's just a nickel.

> **Quick: How much change do you get back from $20.00 if you spent $11.25? Now ask your child the same question.**

Labeling Maps

Purchase an unlabeled map of the United States at any teacher's supply store. Make copies of the blank map and ask your children to label each state. Can they do this? Ours couldn't, at first. Now they not only label the map perfectly, they spell all the states correctly and label capitals, major lakes and rivers, mountain ranges, and historic locations. This can be an entire geography course in itself. How about a world map? Does your child know where the major international cities are located?

Soon after we completed this task, our oldest got his driver's permit. We packed up and drove to the Grand Canyon. Knowing their United States map provoked our sons' interest in traveling to some of the places they had labeled. Camping and homeschooling were great fun, too. You might read *Improve Your Survival Sklls,* by Lucy Smith. Try some of the supplements for mapping listed below:

> *Mapping the World by Heart,* by David Smith (comes with a video)
>
> Name That State, from Educational Insights (a board game)
>
> *Geography Songs Book & Cassette,* by Kathy Troxel

States & Capitals Songs, Map, & Cassette, by Kathy Troxel

Maptitude Game, from Resource Games (a board game)

Take Off! from Resource Games (a board game)

Discover America, from Second Avenue Creations (a board game)

Geo-Safari Talking Globe, from Educational Insights

Life Lessons

We not only thought that textbook learning was important but also life lessons. It's essential that your child learn some of the valuable life lessons only a parent can teach. Here is a list to which you can add. You would be surprised how many teenagers can't do the following tasks:

Clean an oven

Change a tire

Prepare a meal

Paint a room

Tell time without digital clocks

Give directions

Read a ruler

Pull weeds

Know phone etiquette

Write a check

Shut the electrical power off

Read a map

Shut off the main water line

Understand types of insurance

Balance a checkbook

Sort and wash clothes

Fix a leaky pipe

Clean a toilet

Prepare a budget

Introduce someone

Hook up a computer

Change bed linens

Address a letter

Groom a pet

Prepare a shopping list

Listen when others speak

Change a baby's diaper

The Fine Arts

Should my child have music lessons?

This is something we wanted our children to experience. If

you don't play a musical instrument yourself, find a music teacher. Let your child choose the instrument and listen to her practice. If money for music lessons is not available, purchase an inexpensive recorder to learn the notes of the scale. Let your child entertain you while you go about your chores. Think of it as band practice.

Music is a necessity of life. Encourage your child to sing, dance, or listen to all types of music. When we studied history we included the music of each era as part of the course. Music added so much to our homeschooling day. Play soothing music during any subject that causes stress for your children, and watch their attitude change. Play fast, upbeat music during their keyboarding course. It helps them type faster.

Check to see if your support group has a homeschool choir and band. We had a wonderful band conductor who volunteered her time. We may have had an imbalance of brass instruments at first, but we shared a common interest in playing music.

Are theater and drama available to the homeschooler?

You may have to enroll your child in drama classes at your local playhouse, acting school, dance and theater studio, YMCA, or any other organization that would make these courses available. Some curricula provide theater courses, but because theater requires interaction among several players, the courses were limited. Check your homeschooling newsletters or newspaper bulletin listings for available theater courses.

Awards for the Student

Can I give my homeschooler awards or certificates of achievement for certain tasks?

Yes, of course. We gave our children certificates or ribbons for memorizing passages such as the Gettysburg Address, or the states and their capitals. Certificates can be designed on the computer or purchased from any local office supply store. We even found terrific ribbon awards from Wal-Mart and the craft places in our area.

Why not give your children tokens of achievement? You're their teacher, they're your students. Show your appreciation by occasionally giving them a reading certificate for books read, or an incentive sticker on a well-written book report. Who knows, they might present you with an apple one morning!

In Summary

You should have a fair assessment of the level at which to begin homeschooling your child after testing his reading abilities. It should be a comfort knowing that you can tailor a curriculum to fit your child's particular needs. Hopefully, we have enlightened you as to the importance of life lessons in the grand scheme of providing a well-rounded home education. The world of home-schooling is revealing itself to you in more ways than you thought possible.

CHAPTER 5

Getting Down to Business

Taking the First Steps

Let's put the wheels in motion. Many before you have paved the way for homeschooling. They've fought long, hard battles to pass the laws that make homeschooling available to you. Feel excited about beginning a different type of education, one that will make sure your child doesn't get lost in the shuffle.

Withdrawing Your Child from School

How do I withdraw my child from school?

Start by knowing your individual state's homeschooling laws. Check the http://www.hslda.org Web site. Based on those laws and the information you have acquired from your research, follow these steps:

- If your state requires you to fill out a form with the Department of Education, make arrangements to do so.

- If your state requires you to enroll in an existing and registered private home education school, make arrangements to do so.
- If your state requires you to file with the school district an annual letter of intent to homeschool, make arrangements to do so.
- If your state requires you to file with the superintendent of schools in your district that you intend to homeschool, make arrangements to do so.
- If your state considers homeschools as private schools, consider yourself in a "homeschool-friendly" state. The state has no jurisdiction over homeschools, so it will be quite simple.

At the most, if your state requires yearly enrollment through the Department of Education, you'll supply basic information about each child's name, age, parents' names, addresses, which parent will do the teaching, and what public school the child would have attended. A yearly assessment may also be requested for each child.

Each state clearly defines what it expects of homeschooling families. Once you have completed the necessary required documentation, create your own records for your child. Your child's file should contain immunization records, testing results, and any other pertinent information you deem necessary.

Is there a possibility the school may tell me I can't homeschool my child?

There's always a possibility that it might attempt to say you can't homeschool your child, but it would be wrong, especially if you've met your state regulations. Be confident, smile, and know the law is on your side.

Our Experience with Withdrawing Our Children

Withdrawing our children from school proved to be a simple process. We refer to Texas as a homeschool-friendly state. We were aware of the Texas Open Records Act, which defines a student's records as private, and specifically states that the parents have access to all of their child's records. We politely but firmly informed the admissions office that we had decided to homeschool and wanted a copy of our children's records. It's not necessary to get all your child's records, though it would be good to obtain all the test results.

The school gave us the records with their best wishes for homeschooling. The school clerk was actually very comical about the whole thing, telling us we were the sixth family that week to withdraw our child to homeschool. It was Wednesday. Turns out we were nervous for no reason.

I've heard that my public school system gives parents a rough time when withdrawing their children. What should I do?

Get the true facts from those who have withdrawn their children in your district by calling a local support group. Don't rely on hearsay. If you know what your state guidelines are, you won't experience anxiety about the process of withdrawal.

Public School Records

Are the public school records accurate accounts of a child's education?

No. View the records, but realize that people who hardly know your children evaluated their behavior and academic abilities.

One of our son's records labeled him as a hyperactive child without justification. A notation above his immunization form stated, "Hyperactivity noticed in physical education class." You'll sometimes be surprised at what the records contain. Take them with a grain of salt, and be glad you've decided to homeschool.

If my child hasn't been to public school yet, and I plan to homeschool, do I need to notify the school district of my plans?

Verify whether your state homeschooling laws require you to do so. You might be required to fill out information forms or file a letter of intent with your local school district. If not, there's no reason to notify a school district of your intention to homeschool. Just begin your curriculum when your child is ready to begin his education. Contrary to what some people think, school districts don't have a list of incoming students until they are enrolled.

School Supplies

What supplies do I need to begin homeschooling?

The only homeschooling supplies a child needs is the parent.

This can vary from student to student. Our youngest liked shopping for colorful pencils, folders, special pens, and erasers. Our oldest, however, only used yellow number two pencils and white college-ruled paper.

Below is a list of items we accumulated. As time progressed we needed less and less. You can create your own list based on the courses your child will study.

Table and chairs

Bookshelf for textbooks

Pens, pencils, highlighters, paper

Creative writing blank books

Chalkboard, which we found to be useless after about
    a month

Flash cards

Globe

Encyclopedia books or software

Computer and printer, with extra ink cartridges, of course

Internet access

Backpacks for the library and homeschooling on the go

Sweats and T-shirts, which are great for parents, too

Gas in the car for field trips

Homeschooling Effectively

One of the first steps you must take to homeschool your child effectively is to turn the television off during the day. Don't begin the day by watching television. Instead, plan to involve your homeschooler in preparing a balanced breakfast before opening the first textbook. Sit together as you eat breakfast and discuss your plans for the day. When the dishes are cleared and the kitchen is clean, announce that the school day will begin.

Having a television on while homeschooling is distracting for the child and you. Your child shouldn't compete for your attention, and you shouldn't compete for hers. Appreciate the sound of your child's voice reading to you. Help him to focus on the task at hand. Your child is a unique individual who needs your guidance. Accountability starts with you.

> **Keep the television off during the homeschooling hours.**

Homework or No Homework, That Is the Question!

Virtually everything your child does will be considered as work done at home. We never saw the point of assigning something as busywork just for the sake of giving our children homework. After all, we weren't trying to emulate what the public schools were doing. We were trying to get away from all that.

Call It Independent Work

Sometimes it'll become necessary to assign tasks with deadlines for your child to accomplish. Although we wanted our children to work at their own pace, we did want to stress the importance of deadlines, so we created independent work. Independent assignments were designed to teach responsibility and see how they accomplished work on their own. They consisted of research papers, book reports, or outside reading assignments.

The Importance of Meeting a Deadline

Our youngest asked, "If I don't finish my report by Friday, what will happen?" That was a good question. We told him we had several options. We could give him one grade lower than what he earned, but that didn't mean anything since we didn't base knowledge on a grading system. We could give him more time to complete the report, but that didn't teach him responsibility. So, we suggested he tell us what would be fair to teach him the importance of deadlines. He came up with something unique.

He understood what we were trying to accomplish by relating it to money. He knew if payroll departments didn't meet deadlines, then paydays couldn't be counted on. And if his parents couldn't count on paydays, then he couldn't count on his allowance. So, our son's suggestion was no report on Friday, no allowance.

What did we learn? Our children were smarter than we thought. We also learned never to be late with allowances. After all, a deadline is a deadline!

Keeping Good Records

Should I keep records of what my child learns?

There aren't any guidelines of what records a homeschooler needs to keep. Yes, yearly test results are a must to keep, and immunization records are good to have on file. State documentation copies are a must, but what else? We kept more than what was necessary. As a matter of fact, we've kept every paper our sons have ever written, every note they've taken, and every math problem they've solved, which ultimately takes up valuable attic space. We have kept a bit too much.

The only reason we had for keeping all their work was that it added to our sense of security should we be asked to prove we were homeschooling. It truly wasn't necessary. The standing rule of thumb among homeschoolers is that you need only keep the important papers and those records requested by your state laws.

LYDIA LANE

"I gained an excellent education, confidence and self-reliance, respect for the family unit, strong ethics, love of knowledge, strong interpersonal communication skills, and a positive outlook. As a postsecondary educator, I have experienced, firsthand, the limitations of classroom instruction and the results of public education. Many adults have deficient reading, writing, and mathematical skills. In the classroom there was an obvious burden on my students and me when the student-teacher ratio was inadequate. Homeschoolers of the millennium have so many more resources than what was available to me in the '80s. It is most rewarding and amazing to see the massive growth and acceptance of homeschooling."

Lydia Lane, from California, holds an A.A.S. degree in medical assisting and is a certified postsecondary teacher and certified counselor for the U.S. Space Camp program. In the '80s, Lydia's parents made the decision to homeschool when they were tired of telling teachers that their children were displaying obvious signs of educational boredom and burnout.

"I believe that my parents went from being 'frustrated' to 'fed up' when the public school educators wanted to hold my sister back in kindergarten because of her height, despite that her test scores were up to par," Lydia says. She continues, "In the '80s there were a lot of people who continually challenged me regarding my parents' decision to educate me at home, which in turn taught me to be knowledgeable about what I believe in, so I may confidently support my beliefs."

This strong and independent woman defines herself as a full-time homeschool mom. She is in the process of establishing a home-based business and homeschooling her young son.

Homeschooling More Than One Child at a Time

How do I homeschool more than one child?

Public school teachers with overcrowded classrooms ask that very question. But parents know that raising more than one child happens quite naturally. So, why wouldn't homeschooling more than one child be relatively the same?

Teaching more than one child isn't difficult once you get the hang of being organized. Remember, you're never in a hurry when homeschooling. Try some of these helpful suggestions when homeschooling more than one child.

- While one child works independently or reads, teach a new lesson to the other.
- Depending on the age levels of your children, some courses can be tailored to meet the needs of all your children at the same time.
- One of the things we found most helpful was to have one child work on the computer while the other received individual attention.
- Teach your children how to use their time wisely. They'll learn to work independently during the individual instruction time of their siblings.
- It doesn't hurt to give an older child a set of flash cards to use with a younger child. Both learn patience and understanding as well as their multiplication tables.
- Start earlier in the day with the child who needs more individual attention.

Homeschoolers Learn to Use Their Time Wisely

We were at a homeschool basketball tournament several years ago with about an hour to wait until our children played their next game. As we looked around to see what our team members were doing to occupy their time, we found a junior varsity player giving flash card drills in multiplication to an eight-year-old. There was a six-year-old holding up letters for a seven-year-old to identify, and a ten-year-old read his report on whales to a fourteen-year-old. Not one player was getting into trouble, hanging around the bleachers, wandering around the building, or causing problems. All were dutifully making good use of their free time. Homeschooling takes place anywhere and anytime.

What happens if I get called to serve on jury duty?

This happens more than you think. You'll receive a summons, or letter, telling you to report for jury duty on a specific day and hour. Jury duty is considered a civic responsibility, and there are few exceptions about who may serve. Parents with primary care of young children are excused. You're the primary teacher for your children, so fill that out on the letter and mail it back to the courts.

Do homeschoolers have fund-raisers?

Some homeschooling organizations have fund-raisers for their team sports, physical education supplies, and fees for guest lecturers. Since the burden of financial support for extracurricular activities falls on the individual homeschooling families, fund-raisers are highly effective.

One homeschooling family in our support group conducted a fund-raiser to purchase a computer. The parents decided to let their children sell wrapping paper, cards, and stationery right before the Christmas holidays, earning half the money necessary to purchase their computer, which their parents matched.

Motivating a Child

How do I keep my child motivated?

All parents ask this question, even those who don't plan to homeschool.

Webster's Dictionary defines the word *motivate* as to affect, incite, or impel. If you affect, incite, or impel your children even a little each day, they'll stay motivated to learn.

Having the desire to learn is more than half the battle in succeeding.

We live in a world where it seems everything has to be short, sweet, exciting, and to the point. Sorry to disappoint them, but we taught our children that everything isn't short, sweet, exciting, and to the point. There are some pretty boring and mundane tasks that all of us go through in our daily lives.

It's our job as parents to discover how our children learn best and how to help them to achieve. It's not our job to make sure everything is new and exciting. It just doesn't work that way. But how do we do this and keep them motivated? One of the things that worked for us was to provide supplements on topics of interest to them. We show you how to create supplements for your child in chapter 9. If we just could have motivated them to keep their rooms clean, we would have been truly successful.

How do I keep myself motivated to teach?

You get plenty of rest, relaxation, and exercise so you can maintain a level of needed energy each day. Take up a sport, jogging, meditation, prayer, yoga, or even walking in the evening. It'll do wonders for the mind fatigue and give you a fresh outlook for the next day. More important, join a homeschooling support group.

If you're going to be the primary teacher for your child, it's important that you have contact with adults sometime during your week. Teaching children and caring for the home takes its toll on even the best-organized mom. To stay motivated you'll want to pursue extracurricular activities of your own. Join a church group, play Bunco with the neighbors, take walks with a friend, sign up for a class at the community center or college, but do something for yourself.

Homeschooling 8:00 to 3:00

What time should we begin school?

We've been asked by homeschooling families and nonhomeschoolers what time our day began. We found those who homeschooled were doing a comparison study, and those who didn't homeschool were just curious.

There are skeptical nonhomeschoolers who assume if you don't have school during the same hours as the public school, you just aren't educating your child. What we accomplished in one hour would amaze those people.

So What Time Is the Right Time?

You pick the hours. Homeschoolers adhere to schedules that work best for their families.

Our children, like us, had been used to a regimented schedule of getting up early, showering, eating breakfast, then going off to school. We figured if we maintained the same schedule, our children would know we were serious about homeschooling. So by 8:00 we were ready to begin our studies.

> **You pick the hour you plan to begin homeschooling.**

There's no set time. You'll decide what works best for you and your child. As an added piece of advice, the variety of extracurricular organizations available to homeschoolers occasionally involves traveling great distances. We found getting up early and completing our studies allowed for the travel time.

How Many Hours Per Day Should We Homeschool?

How many hours per day should be devoted to homeschooling my child?

We can successfully say that all subjects can be covered in approximately two to four solid hours each day. Don't try to duplicate the public school hours. It isn't necessary. Some days we worked longer to strengthen particular skills. Other days we finished earlier, giving us the opportunity to tour a museum or grocery shop.

Here's a rough estimate of time spent on homeschooling, based on the experiences of several homeschooling families. It doesn't mean you're doing a poor job if you complete your course study in less time.

First through third grade—1½ to 2½ hours per day

Fourth through fifth grade—2 to 3 hours per day

Sixth through seventh grade—2½ to 3 hours per day

Eighth grade—3 to 4 hours per day (several eighth grade homeschoolers were beginning their high school credit hours)

High school—3½ to 4 hours per day (those high schoolers pursuing honors classes in preparation for college were in the 4-hour range)

Year-Round Schooling

Should we homeschool year-round?

This has been a topic of conversation in our support groups for years. Some public schools do have year-round school. Verify if your state requires a specific number of school attendance days. You can then decide whether to homeschool year-round or break for the summer.

We chose to homeschool year-round with fewer courses during the summer months. For about two hours each day, we taught only English, mathematics, and reading during the summer. These were the most important courses to us, so it didn't hurt to keep the skills going during the summer.

Summer Vacations

Many homeschoolers spend their summers vacationing and sightseeing. What better form of education could there be? For those who can't afford that luxury, the library is the next best place. Reading will take your child on exciting tours around the world. If you don't plan to homeschool year-round, at least plan to read year-round.

> **Traveling is homeschooling, too.**

Are You a Morning Person?

I'll never be able to get my child out of bed to homeschool. What do I do?

Be realistic. What time do you plan to start your day? Nobody says you have to begin at sunrise. However, if you plan to begin early, we can give you some tips on getting your child ready to homeschool each day that don't involve throwing cold water in her bed.

- Give your child an alarm clock and teach her how to set it.
- Put your child to bed earlier on the weekdays. A school night should be an important night.
- Be honest. Ask your child how the family would survive if the mother or father couldn't get out of bed to go to work. Everyone must have responsibilities. Age isn't a factor.
- Get your child a pet to care for that sleeps in his room. (A goldfish doesn't count!) Make it his individual responsibility to get up and attend to the pet's needs.

Beginning the Process

I'm not a teacher. How do I begin?

If you're a homeschooling parent, you're a teacher. Start thinking like one.

Establish a place in your home where some of the education will take place. We used the kitchen table. It's not necessary to have school desks and chairs in a special room just for home-schooling, although we know families who have done this. One such family converted its attached garage into its schoolroom. It was quite impressive, with bookshelves, a chalkboard, and even a lab station. (Garth Brooks, the country-western entertainer, and his wife homeschool their children. Garth built them a one-room schoolhouse. Wouldn't that be nice?) You can be as simple or elaborate as you desire.

An Ideal Teacher

You are sitting across from your child. Now what? Well, go and sit next to your child instead. It makes for a better relationship right off the bat. Sitting across from your child screams, "I'm the teacher, you're the student." Sitting next to him says, "We'll learn this together."

You are looking at your book, and your children are looking at you. Now what? Remember those breathing techniques you used in the delivery room? Use as needed, then take one paragraph, one page, one chapter at a time. Go slowly. There's no hurry. What you cover in one day will be more than enough.

How Does My Child Learn?

It really doesn't matter if you know the "official label" of the type of learning style or preference your child exhibits. Don't be concerned with whether your child is an auditory, visual, kinesthetic, analytic, global, linguistic, logical, or spatial learner. Yes, it would be nice if you knew how to reach your child through the most effective teaching tools from day one of homeschooling, but at the start, you don't need that added pressure. This is going to be a whole new way of approaching an education. You need to remember just a few basic things at the beginning.

- Teach slowly; have patience with your child.
- Reteach anything your child doesn't understand.
- Don't move on until your child retains the previous lesson.
- And give words of encouragement every day.

Helpful Hints for Starting

We found reading everything aloud—and we mean everything—to work best. We read the directions aloud while our children followed along in their textbooks, stopping occasionally to explain what we felt needed to be pointed out in detail.

When it came to math, we didn't just assign ten problems and walk away, letting them work them out. We had them do the problems one at a time while we sat and watched or did them, too. This went on for several lessons until they could work independently.

We knew, when they asked too many questions during independent study, we hadn't watched and helped them do enough problems. One-on-one training is what is needed to get started. Even if you only accomplish three math problems or five spelling words in an hour, you're making sure they understand and learn each lesson. Be in no particular hurry to complete a lesson by a certain date. Key into your child's pace. Don't dwell on making the grade. Evaluate your children's progress with how well they are learning. Teach them, but learn with them, too. Never move on until a lesson is retained. Always hug your children every day, and tell them how proud you are of them.

Repeat Courses as Review

Our oldest asked to repeat algebra about six months before he took his SAT for college. We thought that was a good idea, since the SAT's math section is devoted to algebra and geometry concepts. It was amazing how much he had retained, and how fast we traveled through the textbook the second time. It did wonders for his SAT results, too.

Teaching a Course Too Quickly

Don't try to teach an entire textbook in one week. You'll get overly anxious, especially when you see how well the one-on-one training works, and the urge to go over one more thing is going to hit you like a ton of bricks. You'll see your child's skills develop quickly and think "Let's do more."

We felt ourselves doing that very thing several times a year. You get excited at how much your child is retaining. Then you get excited at how well you're teaching. A week later you and your child experience burnout. Slow down. Take little steps per day; giant leaps make for gaps in the fundamentals. Review, review, and review again. Teach for retention. Homeschooling affords you plenty of time.

In Summary

And that's how to begin. You'll continue this method with each course, pacing yourself slowly. The moment you feel rushed, take stock of why you're teaching your children. You're trying to provide a better education than what they were receiving. That was and still should be your goal. Teach your children, but learn with them, too.

CHAPTER 6

The Elementary Years

Kindergarten Through Fifth Grade

The number of elementary homeschoolers who have never attended a public or private school is growing. They've been home-schooled since the first grade. Many of these children will continue to homeschool into their middle school and high school years. Others will enter public middle schools or high schools with fine-tuned fundamentals and superior reading abilities. They'll have the strong foundation skills that all education experts admit need to be acquired in the early years. Perhaps you have an elementary-age child you would like to homeschool. This next section is for you.

Beginning in the Elementary Years

If you're beginning to homeschool during the elementary years, good for you! You won't have to clean up the bad habits your child has acquired from her public school. We so wish we had homeschooled during our sons' elementary years to establish those strong foundation skills of reading and mathematics. Instead, we had to reteach what they should have learned during the elementary years.

During the elementary years a child is eager to learn. Elementary children want to please the teacher. If the teacher is also the parent, it makes for a wonderful relationship. Enjoy this time with your child.

Evaluate Your Child's Situation

Here are some questions to ask yourself when evaluating your child's situation:

- Do you have an elementary school student who leaves school projects and assignments to do until the last minute?

- Does your elementary school student need help with every facet of her homework, giving up easily and being continually disorganized?

- Do you have an elementary-age child failing school?

- Does your elementary school student have so much homework that there isn't much time for anything else in the evening?

- Are you doing some of your child's homework so he gets to bed at a decent hour?

- Has your child's teacher called you more than once this year?

If your child has experienced even one of the above situations, it's time to consider homeschooling. Your child is frustrated and probably weak in the basic fundamentals of reading, phonics, spelling, and mathematics. He's on his way to failing middle school and high school. You have to stop this path of destruction before he totally disconnects from wanting to learn.

It's Just Elementary, Watson!

What do you suggest I read before considering homeschooling my elementary-age child?

There will never be a shortage of helpful books on education, but the topic you want to study the most is homeschooling information. We suggest you start at your local bookstore's educational section to see what is available or meets your specific interests. To get you started, here are a few books that helped us.

You Can Teach Your Child Successfully, by Ruth Beechick (Arrow Press)

Encouragement Along the Way, by Bobbie Howard (Noble)

Children's Book of Virtues, edited by William J. Bennett (Simon & Schuster)

Honey for a Child's Heart, by Gladys M. Hunt (Zondervan) (contains an eighty-five-page list of the best children's classics ever)

How Do You Know They Know What They Know?, by Teresa Moon (Grove) (excellent resource to help evaluate your child's progress)

Teach Your Child to Read in 100 Easy Lessons, by Siegfried Englemann, Phyllis Haddox, and Elaine Bruner (Simon & Schuster)

At what age should I begin teaching my child if she's never been to public school?

Although some states don't require mandatory kindergarten classes for five-year-olds, they do require a child to be placed in school by a specified age. Each state has its own requirements. Check your state's guidelines.

For homeschooling purposes, you'll probably find that your child will be more than willing to begin homeschooling at the age of five or six. If your child is in a preschool or mother's day out program, she's learning colors, shapes, numbers, and some sight words at the age of three or four. She begins learning when she begins asking the never-ending questions like "Why is the sky blue?" That's your cue to begin homeschooling.

What to Teach

What should my elementary student study?

Besides the state-mandated courses, anything that you feel is necessary should be taught. If you have acquired a comprehensive curriculum, textbooks, or supplemental worksheets for first through fifth grade, you'll have nothing to worry about. Just go slowly and teach for retention. Your child will be fully prepared when he begins the middle school years.

If you have homeschooled your child from first through fifth grade, he'll have mastered more than you can fathom. Perhaps you should read the books *What Your 1st Grader Needs to Know* through *What Your 6th Grader Needs to Know,* by E. D. Hirsch. They contain sample texts, poems, and useful information and suggestions about what your child should know in the elementary years. Use these books as guidelines. Then ask yourself if your curriculum is covering enough. Are you teaching so much that your child isn't remembering? Do you need to pay closer attention to what she knows?

Is handwriting a course that I should introduce to my elementary-age child?

Yes. This is an important course. Handwriting courses teach neatness in writing. This is definitely a course for elementary students. Obviously, you'll want to start with teaching your child to print the letters and numbers correctly before you introduce cursive writing.

For younger children use large-spaced note tablets. If the tablet doesn't come with a letter formation chart, obtain a copy of one from your local teaching supply store or curriculum provider.

Phonics and Spelling Tips

What phonics programs are available for my elementary homeschooler?

There are several curriculums that incorporate phonics into their language textbooks. You may have already chosen one. Read through your curriculum thoroughly. If you require a more intense phonics program, try using one of these:

The Phonics Game, by Education Insights, is for grades one through adult. It comes with three easy-to-use videos and seven audio instruction cassettes that help students play each card game along with the video.

American Language Series, by Alpha Omega, introduces your child to phonics with workbooks and cassettes, flash cards, and a spelling manual. It's set at a kindergarten level.

Plaid Phonics, by Modern Curriculum Press, introduces phonics with rhymes, riddles, and pullout cards for grade levels kindergarten through sixth grade.

Patterns and Word Searches

When should I introduce patterns to my child?

Patterns and sequence flash cards are available for the very young and should be introduced during the formative years. The ability to place items, words, numbers, and pictures in patterns is a necessary skill that helps to develop the child's mind in any subject. A child learns patterns when counting to ten or saying the alphabet. Keep those patterns going throughout the entire educational process. Visit your local teacher's supply store and purchase a pattern workbook that is age appropriate for your child. Find at least fifteen minutes a day to work on pattern development in each grade level.

Word Search Practice

Word searches are essential practice work for an elementary home-schooler. They helped our sons with skimming techniques, proofing work, and training the eye to pick out important facts from reading selections. The word search magazines sold at any local grocery store work just fine for practice. Make sure to leave time in your homeschooling week to have your children practice with word searches. They'll think they're getting to play instead of learning. Just don't tell them how educational word searches truly are.

Memorization Skills

Should I have my child begin to memorize facts in the elementary years?

Can you recite the alphabet backwards?

Whether or not he should learn memorization skills is up to you. Elementary students are at the peak of their ability to memorize during those years. They'll easily learn to memorize lists, quotes, states and capitals, vocabulary words, and other things just by working for a few minutes each day. This is one of the reasons small children should probably learn to speak a second language. They remember it so well.

We started with a simple list of the states and their capitals. Putting together a puzzle of the United States is the best way to start learning a memorization technique. By the time children are ready to begin labeling a blank map of the United States, they'll know several states just from doing the puzzle.

What are the positive and negative aspects of teaching a child to memorize using songs and music?

When a child is young, parents teach the alphabet using the standard song "A, B, C, D, E, F, G . . ." and so on. You're probably singing it right this very minute. However, are you able to rattle off every third letter of the alphabet or recite the alphabet

RACHEL HARGRAVES

Rachel Hargraves, from Georgia, is majoring in German at Grace College and will be studying abroad in Berlin next year. This dedicated woman gives an eloquent account of how her family chose homeschooling. A first grade teacher recommended the use of the drug Ritalin, because Rachel stared out the window during class. Rachel comments that by God's grace her parents pulled her out of the public school system, and contemplates what her life would have been like had she been placed on the drug because of something as simple as classroom boredom.

When asked to give her opinion on the positives and negatives of homeschooling, she commented, "Well, for me I was able to study at my own pace. I also enjoyed the variety of subjects that I could study. As for the negatives, I have met many homeschoolers during my time and haven't met any who had anything negative to say about it." She is also eager to point out, "I have been asked too many times to count by non-homeschoolers if I received any socialization. My response was usually that I wished I weren't as socialized. I was always doing something with one support group or another."

After the Columbine massacre touched America's heart, Rachel and her fiancé decided that when they have children, if a Christian private school is not available, they most definitely will choose homeschooling.

backwards? Probably not, and that may have something to do with learning the alphabet through song.

There is something to be said for teaching songs that contain information we want our children to remember. But what about the student who has trouble selecting the letter that follows "U" without mentally singing the alphabet song? The songs work, but you'll want to reinforce them with patterns. That way, you'll know if your child is truly retaining the information learned in the educational songs.

Learning to Write

Should I start a writing program for my elementary homeschooler?

Learning to write is always a good thing to do at any age. Young children will develop good communication skills if they write each day. We suggest you begin by having them write paragraphs or book reports. Move at your child's pace in a writing program.

Speaking Well

Homeschoolers must have a comprehensive language curriculum that enforces the art of speaking well. Not only will elementary-age children profit from learning language mechanics, but also they'll need to learn to speak with clarity, especially if you plan on reentering them in the public schools.

If you encourage your children to ask questions and voice their opinions when they're small, they'll be able to convey their feelings on paper in the middle school years that follow. Plan to read with your children and discuss what you've read together every day. Get them talking and expressing their opinions.

Computer-Age Children

Is it okay to incorporate computer courses into my child's education?

Yes. This is the age of computers. Teach your children to type during the elementary years. Don't wait for high school. If they're old enough to play games on the computer, they're old enough to learn the keyboard. There are several software programs that teach typing, or keyboarding, as it is referred to today. We used *Mavis Beacon Teaches Typing*. This software lets your child pace himself. We recommend that you enforce practice with the home row keys. The software is not capable of monitoring correct finger placement. You'll have to watch the practice once in awhile.

Ask your curriculum provider what computer courses it offers for the elementary-age child. There will be plenty to choose from in each subject.

Physical Education

Should I set up some sort of physical education course?

If your children aren't going to join some type of organization for team sports, dance lessons, or even gymnastics, it would be a good idea to make sure they get some form of physical exercise during their day. Even going to the park, playing on the swings, or riding a bike can be considered physical education. Just make a point of having them do something physical along with their academic studies.

> When was the last time you jogged around the block with your child?

Homeschooling Styles

My child learns best when he sits on my lap and we read together. Is this a good way to introduce homeschooling?

Some very young children learn best when they feel the closeness of their parents. That's perfectly fine. Why would anyone ever want to discourage connection with a parent? We teach to the needs of our children. If they need your arm on their shoulders, provide it. If they need to hear words of encouragement, provide them. You'll do whatever works best.

Now, obviously, trying to teach handwriting from your lap may not work. And, of course, if your child learns to work at his own desk and chair, he'll develop good study habits later in life. Should you wish to homeschool for just a few elementary years before entering your child in a private or public school, it would be a good idea to establish a location for schooling to take place. This will make the transition into public or private schools go smoother.

My child likes to read sitting in her beanbag chair. Is that appropriate?

Sure, why not? Get yourself a beanbag chair and read along with her. Spend hours and hours reading and talking about what you've read together. Wear your slippers and cuddle in a blanket. It's homeschooling; get comfortable.

It's Fun to Homeschool

On Texas spring days we homeschooled outside in the backyard. We took snacks outside with us and used the dogs as backrests. At first, the boys thought they were getting away with something. By the end of the first year, they demanded we go outside for school on beautiful days.

Simplify the way you do school. Grab a pencil and a tablet and sit by the pool, go to the beach, climb up into the hayloft, sit among the flowers, or read sitting on the patio. Be creative and build a homemade tent with the dining room chairs and a blanket under which to homeschool. Lie on the floor and prop your feet up on the couch as you read from a textbook. Stay in your pajamas all day and homeschool. Pretend there's no electricity and homeschool by candlelight. C'mon, parents, don't do what the public schools are doing. It's not working.

Ants in Their Pants!

My child can't sit still long enough to learn a lesson. What do I do?

Your child is the perfect candidate for homeschooling. You'll be able to tailor the "sitting still" time each day.

You need to evaluate whether your child is ready for a structured education. You also need to realize that you may be asking too much of your child by making her sit still for long periods of time.

You'll find the appropriate methods for teaching your child through trial and error. It's not all book learning. Hook up that computer for educational games. Play educational or money counting board games. Use flash cards, draw, paint standing at an easel, go for a nature walk. You'll learn to be creative.

Check to make sure you aren't trying to introduce work that is too advanced for your child. Alpha Omega's LIFEPAC curriculum offers wonderful software and workbooks that are colorful and uncluttered for the elementary-age child. Contact it at 1-800-622-3070 or http://www.home-schooling.com.

Hyperactivity or Attention Deficit Disorder

The school labeled my child as having ADD. Will different homeschooling techniques be necessary?

First of all, we recommend that a medical doctor examine your child. We would not let any school label a child as having ADD, considering that your child might have been bored or more inquisitive than the other children. Let a licensed doctor make the determination. Mention to your child's doctor that you're considering homeschooling. Ask her to help you prepare a curriculum that will work best for your child.

Homeschooling a child with ADD can be a wonderful experience. Without the added stress of performance in the classroom, the child with ADD can excel at her own pace. You can teach slowly, quickly, or whatever your child requires. You can plan lessons filled with outside field trips. You will define a whole new way of educating your child.

The Physically Challenged Child

My child is physically challenged, and I need the best curriculum for her needs. Where do I locate these types of curricula?

You will locate curricula for physically challenged students from most of the curriculum suppliers we have listed throughout this book. Make educated and informed inquiries with your child's medical doctor's help on what is available. The book *Homeschooling Children with Special Needs,* by Sharon Hensley, M.A. (Noble), will help you gain confidence, understanding, and emotional strength and help you effectively teach your child with special needs. Contact the National Handicapped Homeschoolers Association Network for more information:

National Handicapped Homeschoolers Association Network, 5383 Alpine Rd., SE, Olalla, WA 98359

Museums, Art Galleries, the Zoo

Are field trips available for my homeschooled child?

Support groups have a parent who prepares monthly field trips at discounted fees, with name tags and sometimes T-shirts. If you decide not to join a support group, you will prepare the field trips. If you live near a museum district, visit it. If you live near a fire station, tour it. If you live near a wildlife park, hike through it. If you live near an ice cream factory, visit it twice a month.

You decide what is important to see and tie it in with a school lesson, if possible. Our children's favorite field trip was a tour of the live butterfly museum. We wore bright colors to attract the butterflies. Their second favorite field trip was to the IMAX Theater to view educational videos of volcanoes, caves, icebergs, forests, sharks, and many more. We did the same field trips once every two months, just because they liked going. Sometimes the best science lessons are on field trips.

Our support group had a history field trip to a one-room schoolhouse in west Texas. We drove to a remote little town that had saved a historic schoolhouse and rented it out to school tours. We conducted a school day with forty-five students from the ages of five through seventeen. Each carried a chalkboard and was given a *McGuffy* reader. What a fun way to relive the past!

Report Cards

How do I prepare a report card?

We have provided copies for you at the end of this book. Check your state's regulations first. The state may provide you with a form. If you plan to enroll your child in an umbrella school, the school will discuss report cards with you.

We have to admit that during the elementary years and sometimes the middle school years, once you begin homeschooling you won't need report cards. If you can see your child learning each day, you won't need a report of what she's accomplishing. However, records are records, so keep them.

How do I evaluate my child's grades?

Just be fair. Ask yourself, Are your children doing outstanding work and learning everything? If they are homeschooling, they should always be learning everything necessary in each lesson before moving on to the next lesson. Therefore, that is A work. Are they learning almost everything but having difficulty remembering all the work? Don't move on, then, for that is B work. Are they only learning half of what you go over? Then do it again. Homeschoolers should not make C grades. We won't even discuss D or F work.

> Homeschooling isn't about grades.

In the elementary years you can decide whether to give letter grades or satisfactory checkmarks in each subject. Sometimes colorful stickers are all that is necessary to award your child for good work.

Making the Grade

Homeschoolers get asked all the time, "How do you record grades? Does your mom give you all A's?" Homeschooling isn't about grades. Grades don't measure knowledge. It makes nonhomeschoolers angry to hear that most homeschoolers do not grade their children's work. The public somehow feels that if children aren't receiving grades, then they just aren't "going to school."

The only way public schools can keep parents aware of what their children are accomplishing is by enforcing a grading system. The parent, after viewing a progress report or report card, feels part of the educational process. The public school parent assumes the grade reflects retained knowledge. Unfortunately, the system doesn't display some of the following conditions.

> **The best grading system for a homeschooler is to receive a hug from the parent every day.**

- Grades don't reflect all work done in class.

- Grades are based on percentages; tests count as two major grades.

- A's are given for good behavior or having the book in the classroom.

- Zeros are given for days missed until work is made up in class.

- Other students in the class grade homework assignments.

- Grades are set on a curve.

- Papers are not graded in the current semester; therefore, they are carried over.

- Some grades are based on a group effort.

> **Once you begin homeschooling you won't need a report card.**

The best grading system for a homeschooler is to let your child know you're pleased with his accomplishments by giving him a hug in the middle of teaching a lesson. Tell him you are proud of how well he is doing, and brag to the relatives. This applies to middle schoolers and high schoolers, as well.

The School Bus, the Lunch Line, the PTO

Will my child miss riding the school bus, making friends, or participating in school events?

If you are thinking along those lines, homeschooling isn't for your family.

If someone has suggested homeschooling your elementary child because he feels that the public schools are lacking, or his child had a bad experience, you don't have to accept his way of thinking. Let your child go to the public school and find out. Homeschooling is a commitment on your part, and it truly has to be wanted by the parent and child for it to work.

We suggest you give the public school a try in the elementary years if you have any reservations about homeschooling. You can always change your mind the following year. In the meantime, read many books about the educational system and keep a close eye on the work your child is doing in school. Volunteer at the school if you can. You will be the best judge of the quality of education your child is receiving.

Every homeschooler I meet seems to think her children are above average. Are there any normal children who homeschool?

We live in a society that measures worth by grades, awards, clothing, cars, home square footage, and the amount of material possessions one owns (or finances). Everyone wants to brag that his or her child is above the norm. We feel all children have special talents in something. Plenty of so-called "normal" children homeschool. You just need to join a support group so you can meet them.

There are many homeschoolers who have a tough time studying facts, memorizing vocabulary words, and learning to spell, read, comprehend, and write well, and who have a whole bunch of typical learning struggles. Don't worry that your child isn't learning the Gettysburg Address like the four-year-old homeschooler down the street. Don't compare. Take your time; the rewards are worthwhile.

Do we need to spend focused hours without interruption on my child's studies?

> Enjoy your elementary-age children. They won't be little forever.

No. Take breaks to water the garden, read to each other from silly joke books, play with cutouts, build model cars, play Monopoly, bathe the dog, or just talk. You'll have plenty of time to work on the subjects that are required throughout your day. Enjoy each other's time. Enjoy your children. They won't be little forever. We're constantly surprised at how many parents do not enjoy spending time with their children.

Holidays and Vacation Days

Can we take days off that are considered holidays by the public schools?

Sure. It's funny; when the public schools had a day off for bad weather, the public school friends would call our house early in the morning. Our children would then say that their school should be closed as well. We had our share of bad weather days, too. We just didn't know they were bad weather days until friends called.

Do we have to homeschool Monday through Friday?

This is hard to answer with yes or no. Our immediate response is yes. For the school authorities to consider you to be homeschooling, you should be teaching your children every day as if they were attending public school. However, sometimes a day off is well deserved. Or sometimes Fridays are for field trips to the library, museums, or nature walks.

Just remember that Fridays are not for dropping your child off at the mall while other children are attending school. You are asking for trouble with that one. Some states enforce the compulsory attendance laws. For more information on the compulsory attendance laws, you may wish to contact HSLDA. It will provide accurate information in clear, concise terms.

We have met several homeschooling families that teach the Bible in their course selections. Is this required?

No, the Bible is not a required course, nor is it state mandated. Remember, you are the person to decide what courses to teach in addition to the state-mandated courses.

Immunizations

Since my child is not attending public or private schools, do I need to have her immunizations current?

For your child's health you need to have her immunizations current, period. Something you may need to think about, though, is that when your child doesn't attend public or private schools, she tends not to be exposd to childhood diseases; thus, her immune system doesn't build up tolerances to everyday childhood colds, coughs, and the like. This can be good for the child who is sick frequently. However, this can also be a downfall if you plan on entering your child in the public or private school system later. Keep immunizations current.

Reading for the Elementary Student

At what age should I start my child in a reading program?

As soon as he can recognize the McDonald's sign, start a reading program.

Our children learned words just by grocery shopping. Words like *exit, in, out, return, ladies, men's, stop,* and *go* are all available on signs for the three-year-old to view. Gather some picture books at the library, move on to the sight word books, and take it from there. Children will develop a love for books if you guide them.

Children love to do what Mommy or Daddy does. Read in front of your children. Show them that it is an important thing to do. The book *Teach Your Child to Read in 100 Easy Lessons*, published by Simon & Schuster, is for grade levels K–1. It enforces the DISTAR method of using twenty minutes a day and professes that in one hundred teaching days, you can bring your child up to a second grade reading level. It's a way to start if you don't know where to begin.

> How much time does your child spend reading? How much time does your child spend watching television?

I have a child who doesn't like to read. What do I do?

Make sure that your child doesn't have physical difficulties, like poor eyesight, making it frustrating to read. If everything is fine physically, find subjects that interest your child. Choose appropriate reading level books that reflect the subjects your child likes.

For the child who absolutely hates reading, we suggest that you choose books one or two levels below your child's level to start a reading program. If it's easy to read, he'll want to read more. Make it easy and fun to start your child on a reading program, and have your child read aloud to you daily.

Enforce the Reading Course

Reading is a necessity in every subject. You want your child to succeed? Teach him to read. Always have books in the house. Have plenty of books on your coffee table, on the counter, on the hearth of your fireplace, on your child's nightstand, in the bathroom, and on the porch. Make books available to your child at all times.

The other issue that we need to stress is the fact that your children must see you reading. It won't help to tell them they have to read to succeed if they never see you reading. Even if your child only sees you read the newspaper or your favorite magazine, that's fine. Just read in front of her. Take time to stop and read signs in stores with your children. Take time to read labels on packages you purchase when you're with your child. If children see that reading is essential, and their parents rely on reading information about products, they'll know they need to read before they buy or sign something.

Are magazines okay to teach good reading skills to my child?

Sure; there are plenty of children's magazines such as *Highlights* or *Ranger Rick*. Order a subscription for your child if she has an interest in a particular one. Our children loved *Ranger Rick*. We used it as a science supplement. Its photographs are wonderful. Find magazines that your child can read.

I have a child who loves to read. As a matter of fact, I have to tell my child to put the book down and play outside. What do I do?

You thank your lucky stars. Every parent wishes she had a reader. You'll have no problem homeschooling if you have a child who thrives in his reading course. Give him research to do. If he loves to read, chances are he'll love to learn how to research.

It's also a good idea to enroll your children in some extracurricular sports or activities to prevent eyestrain, get them out of the house, give them exercise, and help them discover all aspects of life.

How to Encourage a Nonreader to Read

We didn't have sons who enjoyed reading. So, we decided to give them books that would thoroughly provoke their interest. We gave our twelve-year-old *The Client* by John Grisham, and told him he needed to read one chapter a day during silent reading time. He complained until he read the first chapter. Then he finished the book in two days on his own time.

When we asked our son why this book captured his attention, he replied, "Well, of course, it was a mystery. I felt like you were giving me an adult book to read instead of a kid's book. But, best of all, the lead character was close to my age. Oh, and you finally picked a book I liked." Well, our thanks to John Grisham.

Sit Still

Our sons used to complain that reading was tough for them because it meant they had to slow down, sit still, or "chill out" for an hour. They were much too active to want to slow down during the day. The answer was found: We looked for books that were suspense filled or sports oriented. Then we shut off the television an hour before they needed to be in bed. Last, we told them they could stay up as late as they wanted if they were reading. For our family, it worked. You will find ways to encourage your child to read that work for your schedule. Look for books that will interest them, not you.

My child loves to read books in a series. Is that permitted?

> A homeschooler's first form of I.D. should be a library card.

Sure; encourage any type of reading. Series books have always been popular with children. They love to read and collect series books, feeling they have accomplished great things after reading the entire series. If you have a child who loves to read, you are ahead of the whole ball game. Let her read, read, read.

Make sure that you plan a day for your child to get his own library card. Library cards go hand-in-hand with homeschoolers. It is their first form of I.D.! Our children proudly carried their library cards wherever they went.

What series books do you suggest for my child?

Ask your local bookstore or library to suggest a series that is age or level appropriate for your child before you purchase a whole set. If you haven't been to the children's section of a bookstore in awhile, you're in for a surprise. Bookstores are competing with libraries by providing puppet shows, speakers, performers, and so on. They are the libraries that sell books. Check out the shelves of series books.

The libraries and bookstores do an excellent job of presenting books in a series. Have your child read at least one set of series in her elementary years. It'll give her a sense of accomplishment.

What type of poetry should I introduce to my elementary homeschooler?

You've been introducing poetry to your children from the time they were born by singing or reading nursery rhymes. Ask your librarian to suggest simple, short, humorous poetry as a beginning. Try reading Shel Silverstein's poetry. Our children loved *Where the Sidewalk Ends*. His poetry is humorous and an excellent place to begin a poetry course for your homeschooler.

Could you recommend some books I can read that will keep me motivated while teaching my elementary-age child?

Here is a short list of books you can read. We recommend you browse the local bookstores for topics that interest you. Look through the educational section in bookstores and libraries.

Being Your Best: Character Building for Ages 7–10, by Barbara A. Lewis

A Teacher's Guide to Being Your Best: Character Building for Ages 7–10, by Barbara A. Lewis

Challenging Projects for Creative Minds, by Phil Schlemmer, M.Ed., and Dori Schlemmer

Playing Smart: A Parent's Guide to Enriching, Offbeat Learning Activities for Ages 4–14, by Susan K. Perry

Manipulatives

What type of flash cards should I prepare for my elementary-age child?

You can prepare index cards or just strips of paper as flash cards for learning numbers, addition, subtraction, multiplication, division, letters, traffic signs, symbols, word blends, sight words, colors, shapes, animals and their babies, artwork, presidents' faces, states, countries, flags of countries, flowers, historic sights, and anything else you wish your child to learn. Children between the ages of six and eleven will probably have just as much fun creating the flash cards as using them.

Go to any teacher's supply store and view all the options with manipulatives available for your elementary homeschooler. Don't hesitate to check out the sequence flash cards. They are wonderful learning tools.

What do I do with the elementary-age child who is ready for middle school subjects?

Plain and simple, teach him. Homeschoolers excel at their own levels. Some homeschoolers are way ahead of where they would be if they were in public or private schools. Stop measuring your children with public school standards. Let them move at their own pace.

Don't hold your child back from learning something just because the public school has regulations on when certain subjects should be taught. You are your own school. You are the principal, the administration, and the teacher. Move at your child's pace and enjoy each subject.

Should I use board games as learning experiences?

Yes; spend a whole day or every Tuesday doing nothing but playing educational board games with your child. That is truly what homeschooling affords: the opportunity to mix the day with textbooks and fun educational games.

There are plenty of games on the market that are educational and fun. Visit the Discovery Store nearest you for some unique games and puzzles. Puzzles are a wonderful addition to homeschooling. We suggest that you incorporate Lego's into your learning, too. Teach your little one to play chess. It is a good thought-provoking game of decision and strategy. All these games provide wonderful hours of concentration.

On those days when motivation is needed, or it is raining, pull out a board game. Anything from Monopoly to Scrabble is educational and fun. And, remember, some days just need to be fun. It is a reminder of why you homeschool when you have an entire day of coloring or painting by numbers with your child.

Where do I store all the school supplies in our home?

When you figure that out, let us know. We have invested in more plastic containers than we care to admit. We have bookshelves in every room of our home, and we're working on the garage. The attic is full of work the children have done. You'll just have to learn to live with the additional clutter.

You don't have to save everything, just the important things. Every paper our sons did had sentimental value for us, although we have to admit, since the oldest has been in college we have thrown a bunch out. We're hoping that when the children are older and have places of their own, they'll take what's left of their schoolwork with them. Fellow homeschooling parents have told us not to count on it.

Reentering Public or Private School

How do I prepare my homeschooler for a transition into a private school?

We talk about the transition from homeschooling to public or private school throughout this book because it is an important topic. If you find yourself having to place your elementary child back in a public or private school, there definitely will be an adjustment period. If possible, always enter your child at the beginning of a school year, or at least the beginning of a school semester.

Your child will need to learn to raise her hand, stand in line, wait her turn, and have scheduled bathroom breaks. Individual attention on her schoolwork is limited. You're going to have to schedule a parent/teacher conference before your child begins and discuss your concerns. A good teacher will understand what your child is going through and offer advice to make the transition less cumbersome. It will be your job to make sure your child's teacher is aware that you don't expect a quick fix. You just want the teacher to be compassionate during the transitional phase. Your child might voice some of the following comments:

"The other children are mean and push and shove."

Relax. Let your child adjust to the hustle and bustle of school. Just make sure to listen to what your child is saying. In today's world pushing and shoving will be handled by the teacher when witnessed. The school systems have to toughen up on what is tolerated. If it sounds like unusual aggression, do not hesitate to go see what is going on.

"I get hungry before lunchtime."

It takes time for this adjustment. Perhaps you could send a snack for the entire class once in awhile if the teacher permits.

"I have to let the other children answer some questions, too."

This one makes us smile. We have friends who are teachers, who have commented that they wish all their students had at least one year of homeschooling. After one-on-one homeschooling takes place, your child will be able to answer almost every question in class. And, yes, your child may get frustrated that the others do not respond as much.

"It's too noisy."

There is a lesson to be learned for all homeschoolers: Don't try to homeschool in complete silence—sort of like that advice

Grandmother gave about not vacuuming when the baby is asleep, because it will wake the baby. Make noise while the baby sleeps, or the baby won't learn to sleep through anything.

"I have to sit all day in one chair."

It might feel this way to your children at first, but they will soon realize that they get to go to lunch and recess, and do other things. Give them time to adjust.

In Summary

Homeschooling during the elementary years can be so rewarding. Your child's developing a love for reading is an even bigger reward. Making the decision to homeschool during the elementary years will provide your child excellent foundation skills, something needed to succeed in the middle and high school years.

So, what's it going to be? Are you ready to homeschool that first grader, third grader, or fifth grader? Sit back and we'll guide you through the middle school years.

CHAPTER 7

The Middle School Years

Preteen Years, Emotional Years

The middle school years are the most emotionally difficult for students. Peer pressure can be overwhelming, and the emotional ups and downs take their toll on students and parents. If you've withdrawn your child from public school during these years to homeschool, you aren't alone. We've met many a family that made its decision to homeschool during the years of sixth, seventh, or eighth grade.

These are the years that display all the gaps in your child's education, if you're in tune to the signs. Grades don't decline just because your child is emotional. They go down when your child feels defeated or unable to complete a

Grades don't decline just because your child is emotional.

task. You might think children are being lazy in their schoolwork, but in reality, they're shutting down. They have gaps in their foundation skills, and those foundation skills are very much needed in the middle school years. If your child fits into this category, you have several questions.

This can be a trying time for parents watching their children struggle with the emotional turmoil, let alone the academic struggles, that arise during the sixth, seventh, and eighth grade years. One of the toughest situations for a middle schooler is the transition from friendly elementary teachers to strong-disciplined middle school teachers. Sixth graders change classes every fifty minutes, use school lockers, and have four minutes to get to their next class. They panic the first semester of the year and take that stressful attitude into the classroom. Now, pile on poor academic skills, and that spells trouble. And trouble creates bad attitudes toward the teacher, the parent, and the schoolwork. Stress is a big factor in whether a child learns properly.

By homeschooling during the middle school years you'll alleviate the stress in your child's life and place the emphasis on learning. This is a good time to begin homeschooling if your child is lacking strong academic skills. Whether you choose to homeschool one year out of the middle school years or through high school, this chapter will benefit you greatly.

Where Did They Go Wrong?

Stress is a big factor in how a child learns.

Your child's decline in academics didn't happen overnight, suddenly making the middle school years difficult. If we could somehow look back in time and spy on your child's education, we might find that the fundamentals were interrupted and not given the fullest teaching attention because they were taught by a substitute, or there was a fire drill, or a pep rally was scheduled, or there was a discipline problem that took teaching time away. All of that really doesn't matter at this point. What matters is that you're going to reteach the skills your child didn't master by homeschooling.

Caution: Teenager in the Room

How will I know what courses to teach my middle schooler?

You should have your list of required subjects from your state organization and have made plans to obtain curricula based on those subjects. Always stay within the law and teach what is required first. Pay close attention to the subjects that your state mandates, like English, mathematics, reading, spelling, science, and social studies.

Contact the Home School company and ask for one of its catalogues. This company is run by experienced homeschoolers who will answer your curriculum questions. It features a wonderful list of books, textbooks, and workbooks to go with your chosen curriculum. You can reach it at: The Home School, P.O. Box 308, North Chelmsford, MA 01863-0308, 1-800-788-1221, http://www.the homeschool.com.

The Emotional Middle School Child

How will my middle school child feel about homeschooling?

Ask him. Sometimes it depends on the reasons why you are homeschooling. If your child had problems conforming to the group, or caused problems at school, he might try the same with you. It'll take some getting used to. Don't try to do everything the way the public school did. You may feel the need to do this at first, just because you don't know any better. But it won't take long to set up your own teaching and learning methods.

If you create a loving as well as learning environment, your children will feel powerful in their attained knowledge. Children who feel intelligent and proud of their accomplishments become well-adjusted adults. Don't worry that you pulled them from public school during the middle school years; they'll do just fine. You'll need to reassure your children that you're there to help. Don't make them feel bad because of skills they haven't mastered.

We found that several needed skills had never even been introduced to our children; it wasn't a matter of them not paying attention in class. Be patient. Don't hurry. Go slowly over the fundamentals. One day at a time will develop into a month, two months, and before you realize it, a year will have gone by.

The Middle Schooler's Social Life

Should I be concerned about my child's social life?

It is true that children like to be around other children, teenagers like to be around other teenagers, and adults like to be with other adults. However, if you think that your child will lack a social life just because you choose to homeschool, you're mistaken. Only those people who don't homeschool believe this theory. Homeschooling separates education from socializing only during the teaching hours. We're sure you don't plan on locking your child in his room for the rest of the day.

By joining a support group or extracurricular sport or activity, you'll provide your children with social skills. Believe us, you'll soon have a house full of homeschoolers, public school children, neighbors, and friends if you have a teenager. Your child will never be at a loss for a social life.

Assure your child that you're there to help her.

My middle schooler is so emotional. Will this affect the homeschooling process?

The emotional ups and downs that are associated with the teen years will always be there, no matter if you send your child to public, private, or homeschool. As parents, you'll learn to deal with the emotions. Some teenagers have a crisis every morning in selecting what to wear to school. Already, by homeschooling your teenager, you'll have eliminated the "what to wear" crisis before it begins. One problem solved, two thousand to go.

A dear homeschooling friend gave us a piece of advice that we've used endlessly. She said, "When raising teenagers, it'll seem as if they're continually riding a roller coaster. The trick is not to get on the roller coaster with them." That's excellent advice. Stay on the ground and watch them ride the roller coaster. They always return to the same spot where you'll be waiting.

Gas Up the Car, You're the Chauffeur

It appears that if I want my child to have extracurricular activities, I'll have to make that happen. Is that true?

Yes, it's a fact. You'll have to drive them to the extracurricular activities. You'll possibly coach the team sports. You'll have to conduct the spelling bees. You'll have to volunteer. Your title is growing from parent to teacher to chauffeur and maybe coach.

You have children; well, the social concerns go hand-in-hand. But, guess what, whether you homeschool or not, you are responsible for your child's social life anyway. When they're small you introduce new friends and ideas when they join groups like Little League or Girl Scouts. It won't be any different.

The only difference will be that your child won't bump into any other students during school hours. He won't go to lunch with another student during his day, and nobody will smack him around in the middle of language class. He'll be learning during the homeschooling hours without interruption. Best of all, he'll have one-on-one training and excel at his own speed. Socializing will come after school during the extracurricular activities. There's nothing wrong with that concept. Don't let anybody tell you there is.

My middle schooler can be so rude. Is this normal behavior for all middle schoolers?

No. So many parents take the easy way out when having to correct their children. They blame the child's age, emotional state, or friends. Enough is enough, we say. If your child is rude to you and other people, it's time to teach him proper behavior. If you

MATTHEW OTIS

"I feel the prospective homeschooler should have the opportunity to hear the pros and cons of homeschooling presented in a non-biased format as much as possible. No family should be persuaded to homeschool. Homeschooling can be an extremely positive experience, but it has a high cost. The parents must be willing to give as much to the homeschooling effort as their children are willing to give. This is a joint venture."

Matthew Otis currently attends Texas A&M University, majoring in biomedical engineering. He hopes to be involved one day in the making of robotic prosthetic equipment.

Although Matthew has the utmost respect for the educational value homeschooling provided, he does admit that he missed being able to play organized team sports. He feels this is an important aspect of a teenager's life in socialization and peer interaction, and requests that prospective homeschoolers weigh the options based upon their child's needs. "Although homeschooling has helped many children, it is important to also realize that many of those children would do well in the public sector if the parents chose to take a more active role in the child's education."

When asked if he would homeschool his children one day, Matthew replied, "At this time in my life, I would have to say that because the social interaction and team sports were important to me, I don't think I would choose homeschooling for my child. Seeing the time my parents put into homeschooling me also leaves me wondering if I would be able to dedicate the necessary time to make homeschooling successful. I think I would be more inclined to interview private schools that offer high academics, team sports, and a safe environment."

haven't been doing this through the elementary years, it's time to start.

In addition to teaching your child's curriculum, begin by teaching your middle schooler how to make introductions. She'll need this skill when joining homeschooling groups. Many young teenagers don't even know how to introduce one

> Teach your middle schooler to make introductions. She'll need that skill in the homeschooling world.

friend to another, let alone introducing an adult to another adult. Teach your children to speak clearly, shake hands, and be polite. Homeschoolers must get along with all ages. You'll find that your child's communication skills will improve as you share conversation during your learning day.

Report Cards

How do I prepare a report card for my child? Is it even necessary?

Preparing the report card is the easy part. Whether or not it's necessary is going to be up to your state's requirements. There's a sample in the back of this book for your convenience. You can create a report card on your personal computer and modify it to fit your child's grade, or you may simply photocopy our designs and use them for yourself.

A report card is just a report *for other authorities* on how well your child is progressing. You can keep his grades in a journal and submit a copy only when necessary. Verify if your state requires you to submit your child's grades to a particular authority.

Learning Is Retaining

Children take pride in their work. You're the only one who will be able to fairly assess your child's progress. You may want to reread the section on grading your child fairly in chapter 6. In the middle school years we chose to use the grading scale that the public schools used. We felt an A in a course meant our children were re-taining and mastering everything in that course. That should be the goal. All other work was either satisfactory or redone.

Grading Fairly

How can I grade my child fairly?

Relatives and neighbors have asked us how we fairly as-sessed our children's progress. This is why we used the pass/no pass system. Either our children understood the lesson, or they didn't. If they didn't, we worked on the lesson until they did; there-fore, they always did A work.

> **A homeschooler should always do A work.**

You don't have an administrator de-manding that your children progress at a certain pace. Take your time. Make sure they understand everything. When you finally give them a test for a grade, they'll automatically earn a high score if they've learned what they should have. We didn't test them until we were sure they knew what they were doing. Isn't that how learning was intended to be?

If you choose to work under an umbrella school, it will pre-pare the report cards for a small fee. It will, however, need you to supply the grades for the recording.

> **Don't let a twelve-year-old make the decision of what's best for her educational future.**

My child isn't sure whether he wants to homeschool. What do I do?

Would you let a two-year-old decide when to go to bed? Of course not. You know he needs his rest to grow healthy and strong. Don't let a twelve-year-old make a decision on what's best for her educational future, either. If your child can't read in the sixth grade, he won't read any better in the seventh grade without your help. You are responsible for him receiving a good education and becoming an independent adult, even if he remains in the public school system.

You are the parent. Make the decision based on the best educational plan for your child. Your child didn't decide whether to go to public or private school. When you homeschool it has to be for a reason. What is your reason? Think long and hard about the best plan of action.

Yearly Testing Requirements

Should I have my child tested each year?

Your state may require that your child be tested yearly. Check your state's homeschool guidelines. However, though we lived in a state that didn't require mandatory testing, we chose to test our children each year. The testing was a judgment call on our part to see how they were prospering and how well we were teaching. Whether or not to test your child yearly in a state that doesn't require testing is entirely up to the parent. For testing information, contact Bob Jones University's testing facility at 1-800-845-5731.

Homework for the Middle Schooler

In public school the homework level was endless. How will I know if I'm giving my middle schooler enough schoolwork to accomplish?

Why give them homework at all? Stay away from the public school thinking. Although the original concept of homework was as extra practice of skills learned in class, it no longer seems to be for that reason. Ask your children why they have homework. You'll hear the following responses:

"Oh, because we were talking in class, and the teacher got angry."

"There wasn't enough time to finish the lesson in class."

"We had a substitute who assigned the homework."

"The teacher said, since we didn't understand the lesson in class, we should ask our parents to help us."

"Our teacher said we have to have homework every day so our parents don't think we aren't accomplishing anything."

We have always said that if the public school teachers knew who was really doing the students' homework, they might understand why the students were failing. We were constantly helping and actually doing some of our children's homework each day. We simply felt we had to if we wanted our children to have a decent night's rest. The homework was nothing but busywork, but then we didn't realize that until we homeschooled. As you can plainly see, there's no need for homework when homeschooling.

Specific Middle School Course Suggestions

Can I teach additional courses to my middle school child along with the state-mandated courses?

Sure; this is encouraged. As we mentioned earlier, we gave our children their typing course in their elementary years. Teach what is required by your state, then teach what their hearts desire.

Some parents supplement curricula with research they've done to enhance a particular subject. We did this on several levels. During the presidential election we prepared a supplement to use with their history and government books just by doing some simple research at the library and on the Internet. We also suggest that you meet other homeschoolers and share thoughts on what works best.

Mathematics

On what mathematics concepts should my middle schooler be working?

Basic mathematics concepts will be covered by any comprehensive curriculum, including but not limited to groups of numbers, common math symbols, properties of mathematical operations, order of operations, place value, percent, decimals, fractions, formulas, scientific notation, powers, roots, exponents, measurement, graphs, probability and statistics, variables, and word problems. Prealgebra concepts can be introduced in the seventh or eighth grade, depending upon the ability of your child.

Take the time to go over mathematics lessons your child doesn't completely understand. In other words, if a lesson is difficult for your child, stop and create extra practice worksheets to enforce that particular concept. Don't move on until she retains the information.

Health

Should I teach health to my middle schooler?

This may be a requirement of your state. Check the guidelines for your particular state. Even if it isn't a requirement, health is an excellent subject to introduce to the middle schooler. This is a necessary course for the young teenager, and it can incorporate a drug and alcohol awareness supplement. Many parents choose to teach this course in the seventh or eighth grade year.

Literature

Should I be planning a course for my middle schooler in literature?

We thought teaching literature was a good idea, especially for the student who was planning to study advanced high school classes in preparation for college. You really don't have to research what to teach if you use a suggested literature textbook to go along with your child's language program provided by a comprehensive curriculum.

Literature is certainly a good way to teach language and reading. Knowing what pieces to read is another matter, especially if you never enjoyed reading the classics. Ask other homeschoolers what worked best for them. There are plenty of books at your local bookstore and library that list suggested authors and literature for your middle schooler.

Geography

How important is geography for the middle schooler?

Although many states don't require geography to be taught in each year of the middle school education, it's important that your child be able to identify maps, read maps, know time zones, and be familiar with other cultures.

We suggest purchasing or, if your child is artistic, drawing and making copies of blank world maps to label. Your child should be able to label world time zones, United States time zones, the continents, and bodies of water. What you choose to teach otherwise will be up to you and the textbook or supplements you use.

Foreign Languages

My middle schooler is asking to learn a foreign language. What do I do?

> When a child asks to learn a certain subject, it should be taught.

Teach it! When a child asks to learn a particular subject, it should be taught. If you are worried you can't teach the foreign language she's requested, don't despair. There are videos, tapes, other homeschoolers who speak the language, textbooks with teacher's manuals, and software programs that will assist you with a foreign language. Take advantage of all the materials available to teach a foreign language, and learn it with your child.

Where do I find a foreign language tutor for my child?

Ask another homeschooler. Ask this question at your support group meeting. You might find another parent who is fluent in the language of your child's choice. Call a tutoring center. Call your local private school and ask if it has a tutor available. Call the community colleges and ask if they have a college student available for tutoring. Call a foreign language club in your area. Put a notice up at your church or community center advertising your needs. Keep asking; you'll find one.

High School Credits

Can I give my middle schooler high school credit for a course?

Certainly you can, and you should. How about typing, which you taught him in seventh grade, or the algebra course you completed in the eighth grade? All can be recorded as high school credit. We don't recommend that you record it as credit until your child's eighth or ninth grade report card, though. Just save the documentation and enter it on her transcript at the high school level.

Can my middle schooler be in several course levels at the same time?

Yes. You may have a son who is in seventh grade math and ninth grade language. Or a daughter may be beginning her ninth grade math course for credit, but be in her eighth grade science book. Take your time. Teach for retention. Do not classify your child by saying that she's thirteen, so she must be in the eighth grade studying all eighth grade subjects. It's very important, however, that your child be able to read at the grade level of the course he is studying.

Da Vinci, Renoir, Picasso, and Rauschenberg

How do I teach my child art if I'm not very creative?

There are plenty of art courses and art books available from drawing to art appreciation, for the parent and child. You can simply order an art course from the curriculum of your choice and study it along with your child. That works. Remember, we learn together.

We contacted the art teacher at our child's previous public school and asked if she would give private art lessons at her convenience. Your child hasn't experienced an art lesson unless he's had one-on-one training with an artistic person. It was truly wonderful to watch this art tutor express herself. A year later, the art teacher decided to homeschool her daughter and began giving art lessons to homeschoolers in her home.

Here are some books to get you started:

Drawing with Children, by Mona Brookes

Mark Kistler's Draw Squad, by Mark Kistler

Mark Kistler's Imagination Station, by Mark Kistler

The Complete Book of Drawing, by A. Smith and J. Tatchell

The Story of Painting, by Anthea Peppin

Art Adventures at Home, by M. Jean Soyke

Miracle Art: Trick Drawings, by Vic Lockman

Artistic Expression

Remember that art can be something as simple as flower arranging or making favors for a senior citizens home. It can be ironing fall leaves between sheets of wax paper and displaying them on the kitchen window. It can be an hour spent coloring in a favorite coloring book. It's making Christmas ornaments or decorating cookies. It's building model cars and boats, or sewing a quilted pillow. Keep it simple, keep it fun; it's all considered art. Did you ever consider these projects as art lessons? Maybe you should.

- Help Grandma color her hair
- Paint with pudding
- Work with stickers
- Carve a pumpkin

- Learn to wallpaper or paint a wall
- Make shadow puppets
- Design pictures on the computer
- Go to an art gallery for the day
- Put together a 3-D puzzle
- Dye Easter eggs
- Groom a pet
- Decorate the house for a holiday

Drop Down and Give Me Twenty

Remember those words in gym class? How in the world are you going to teach your child physical education? When's the last time you ran a mile?

Don't fret. There are ways to make sure your curriculum includes physical education. Have your children join as many extracurricular sport activities as they wish. Are they on the swim team in your subdivision? Well, that's physical education. Are they taking karate or dance, playing ball, bowling? All are considered physical education.

Let's make one thing perfectly clear: Playing soccer on the Nintendo is not physical education. We, however, place cutting grass and pulling weeds right up there with running, and wouldn't hesitate to call those tasks physical education, too.

Expelled from the Public School

I have a middle schooler who was expelled from public school, so we've decided to homeschool. Can he learn on his own while I go to work?

No. If your child has been expelled from the public school system, there is already a severe discipline problem. Leaving your

> **Just because your child is at home and there are books in the house doesn't mean he's homeschooling.**

child at home, without supervision, is not homeschooling and may make the problem worse.

As the parent, you have to put forth an effort to educate your child. Just because your child is at home and there are books in the house, doesn't mean he's homeschooling. If you're at a loss, read the section on tutoring or private schools again. Homeschooling takes commitment on the family's part.

Should I create a school I.D. for my child?

This is a good idea, for a school identification comes in handy for things like discounts on movie admissions or photo identification when traveling. Most middle school students are given a school identification by their public or private schools. Places like Office Depot and Office Biz can laminate your cards, take passport-style photos, and create the look you want if you don't have the computer or supplies necessary.

Should I have school photos taken each year?

Sure, why not? If you save a scrapbook that shows the growth rate of your child, why not include a school photo? Your child is in school, so create a school photo. We took the boys to the local department store photo labs around the holidays for inexpensive pictures and used them as school photos. You can take the photos yourself and have them made into wallet-size pictures for your children's friends, too.

> **Create a reading list for your children based on what you would like to have them read.**

Is there a suggested reading list for middle schoolers?

Suggested reading lists don't exist in the homeschooling community. Public and private schools have reading lists for

DAN NORDSTROM

Dan Nordstrom, from Minnesota, began homeschooling when his family experienced disappointment with the public school's ability to help his older brother, John, a sophomore at the University of Wisconsin, who had dyslexia difficulties. Dan homeschooled during his elementary and middle school years, choosing to enter public school for the high school years.

Dan's initial adjustment to public high school was a little difficult because he wasn't used to large groups of his peers acting in a silly, rowdy way. His mother, Valarie, proudly says, "He hung in there through those early weeks, and I really admired his courage in making his way through that initial anxiety. It wasn't long until he was a track captain, vice president of the National Honor Society, an editor of the school newspaper, and most impressive, valedictorian of his graduating class."

Dan is currently attending the University of Minnesota, majoring in mechanical engineering. This hardworking young man works summers to pay his own tuition. Dan is thankful for his homeschooling experience when it comes to studying his college-level courses. He realizes that because of homeschooling, he is able to sort through vast amounts of information and teach himself, something most of his peers are finding difficult.

Dan knows that homeschooling helped him find his independence, and that he experienced a stronger and closer connection to his family. His only negative feeling about the homeschooling experience was that his socialization skills, at first, were weak, but he is quick to point out that it was probably due to the reserved sort of person he is. Dan sums up his thoughts on homeschooling by saying, "Looking back, homeschooling has made me realize you only get what you put into it. At the time, I thought I was putting forth ample effort. If I had to do it again, I'd work even harder."

middle school and high school students, but even those lists vary from teacher to teacher. There is no set list for all middle schoolers, but you can create one. We talk more about reading lists and literature selections in the next chapter.

Homeschooling Just for a Year or Two

Is it okay to homeschool for a few years and then place my child back in a public or private school?

Homeschoolers may enter public or private schools with stronger skills and more confidence. Try to enter your child at the beginning of the year or semester, if possible. Some schools will accept the homeschooling grade level as a placement basis. Others will test your child. The majority of schools today are happy to receive homeschoolers because of their excellent academic skills and respectful behavior.

A Note Regarding High School Credits

Those students planning to attend high school at a public or private school should enter as freshmen. High schools will want to test your child. Some states have the right to deny credit and ask the student to retake the class. So, if you have issued high school credits to your middle schooler, you'll have to talk with a school counselor about credit validity.

Homeschooling is a commitment. Make the decision whether to homeschool or not and give it all your attention. Don't move your child in and out of the system without cautious consideration, or you'll be putting up red flags for the public school system to notice.

In Summary

The middle school years don't have to be the emotional years. Homeschooling away from peer pressure may be all your child needs to excel in her academics. Don't be afraid to make the decision to homeschool for a year or perhaps through the high school years, if your child is in need of your help. A middle schooler deserves a chance to excel in school without fear of failure. You are the one to make it happen. Next, let's look at the high school years.

CHAPTER 8

The High School Homeschooler

So You Have a High School Homeschooler!

Either you've made it this far with homeschooling and are now facing the high school challenge, or you're totally fed up with the lack of education your child has received in a public or private school and are just beginning. Either way, this section is for you.

High school students aren't so tough to teach. There are actually plenty of teenagers who want to learn. They are this country's next generation of voters, and they are extremely concerned about the future.

Some parents say they most enjoyed the years when their children were small, but we found the teenage years the most rewarding. It's a joy watching children become adults with educated minds. As parents, you'll know you've done a good job of raising children when they become teenagers confronted with stressful situations and have to make the best choice.

Last Chance to Work on the Fundamentals

Beginning in the high school years gives you the responsibility of paying close attention to more details than in the lower grades. Your child will be earning credits toward a diploma, so you'll need to keep excellent records.

It would be a good idea to test your high schooler for solid fundamentals. If the foundation skills are weak, now is your last and only time to fix everything before graduation. It can be done by working hard. You and your child will need to put forth the energy to bring those skills up to par. Homeschooling in the high school years certainly takes a joint effort between the student and parents.

> **This is your last chance to make sure your child can read and write.**

These Are the Scary Years—Help!

Why are you afraid of these years? It's because you're afraid if you don't educate them properly, they'll never get into college, get a job, and, more important, move out of the house and become responsible adults.

Most parents who have talked with us were thinking of homeschooling their children in the elementary years, maybe the middle school years, but never the high school years. Biggest fear? That they wouldn't be able to teach the higher-level courses and get their children into a decent college. Lose the fear. We're going to help you with the high school years.

What courses are available for my high schooler?

Check your state's list of mandatory courses for the high schooler and the number of credits needed for graduation. Make a list of what classes are a must before you note the elective courses your child would like to study. Get the basics down, order the curriculum for the mandatory classes, and then research the electives.

Courses Available

We were amazed at all the courses available for our high schooler. Instead of just an English course, for example, a homeschooler can specialize within that subject. You and your high schooler will decide what looks appealing to study. For instance, English may include separate courses in grammar, composition, spelling and vocabulary enhancement, American, British, or even international literature, dramatic readings or poetry, creative writing, technical writing and researching skills, SAT practice and analogies, manuscript writing, and contrast and comparison studies. You have the freedom to study individual development courses in the high school years. We found this a wonderful approach to each course. If a child enjoys dramatic readings or poetry, you can devote half a year to that specific subject and still give them credit for the English course.

A mathematics major might choose consumer math, Algebra I or II, geometry, solid geometry, calculus, finite math, probability and statistics, or even computer math and linear functions. How about the child who wishes to major in the sciences? She can choose from biology, chemistry, earth science, physical science, environmental science, meteorology, geology, anatomy, physiology, or marine biology. What about social studies? Your high school homeschooler can study American, state, or world history, geography, government, politics, economics, psychology, sociology, or even anthropology.

Don't Forget the Fine Arts

A student's private or group lessons in music or dance can be recorded as fine arts credit on the transcript. Art, choir, dance, orchestra, drama, speech, or music appreciation can be recorded as credits earned toward graduation.

High School Electives

Electives can include but are not limited to office administration, foreign languages, computer science, accounting, keyboarding, business law, business administration, photojournalism, marketing, and journalism. As you can see, your child won't have a hard time finding courses that interest her.

True or false? Frogs can be dissected on the kitchen table.

Dissecting Frogs at Home

Will I be able to obtain lab supplies for science classes?

Yes, we did our share of dissecting frogs and mixing chemicals. Several curricula sell lab kits and will ship specimens directly to your home.

LYNDEE VISARRAGA

"Benefits of homeschooling? There are so many I don't know where to start. Homeschooling allows any child with a love for learning (and even those with no desire to attend school) to set [his] own pace and receive undivided attention from [his] parents. I loved homeschooling because Mom trusted my desire enough to let me decide what I wanted to learn and let me set the pace for how fast I learned it. I enjoyed every year of homeschooling, and I appreciate my parents' taking the plunge and trying to appease my inquisitive mind."

Lyndee Visarraga's parents chose homeschooling for their daughter when she became apathetic about school. Lyndee acknowledges that she just didn't care anymore about passing. This highly creative woman graduated from Snow College with an associate of arts degree and a major in communications and looks forward to her fall semester at Utah State University. Lyndee loves

If you haven't already contacted Bob Jones University for its catalogue you should do so at http://www.bju.edu/press. It has a wonderful lab kit and specimen setup for homeschoolers. You don't have to use its curriculum to order the specimens.

We found several items, including our telescope, at the Discovery Store. Its employees were most helpful, having a vast amount of educational projects, games, and books.

Contact American Science & Surplus, 3605 Howard Ave., Skokie, IL 60076, (847) 982-0870, for science kits, such as Recreational Chemistry. This is a product of the Smithsonian Institution and claims to be the safest chemistry set made.

How will I teach geometry, or journalism, or physics?

You have the teacher's manual. Learn the course right alongside your child. There's no law that says you must know all the

music and its power to touch human hearts. She composes her own music and has professionally produced one song.

Lyndee's story has a unique twist, one about which many prospective homeschoolers are curious. Beginning in her high school freshman year, she enrolled part-time in public school while homeschooling part-time. She was on the track team and was a member of the speech and debate team, where she earned second place at a competition with a speech about "opposite-sex gym teachers." She went on to sing with the Richfield High School choir as a second soprano, and became a cheerleader. She points out, "The entire four years I was enrolled in high school, I was also attending homeschool part-time. I recommend this style of learning to any child, with one exception. That child has to be confident with who he or she is. Peer pressure is too great in high school and students unsure of themselves can be compromised very easily."

Lyndee looks forward to having children in the future, and she comments, "I definitely plan on homeschooling each one."

answers and be able to work the problems better than your child in order to teach the course. Because of the lack of teachers today, public school teachers often work outside their majors. Public schools are having science teachers teach history and history teachers teach mathematics. That should make you feel better.

Remember When You Were in High School?

Long time ago? Short time ago? Try to remember what it was like for you in high school. Chances are you recall which subjects were troublesome. Think about that for a moment. Were those subjects difficult because your teacher didn't explain things well, or were they hard because you didn't apply yourself? We bet it wasn't because you weren't capable of comprehending. Now, relate all this to your high schooler, and strive to be the best teacher you can be for your child. And when your child doesn't seem to be able to focus on her studies, remember, sometimes her mind will wander just because she's a normal teenager.

Need a Job for That Car Insurance

Learning by doing is attractive to many high school students.

Can I give my high schooler credit for a part-time job?

Yes. Our oldest worked part-time at a retail clothing store to earn money for his car insurance. The manager of the store was happy to provide an evaluation of our son's attitude and work performance for our records. This was a positive experience for our child. We gave him credit for a year of work and listed it as work experience in retail on his transcript.

Before sending your high schooler out to look for a job, cover a small supplement on filling out a job application. She'll be more at ease, having already gone through the procedure at home in a practice interview.

Vocational Courses

Vocational courses are for the homeschooler simply because the homeschooler has the freedom to take courses at vocational school during the day. Consider offering your homeschool high schooler courses in retail merchandising, agriculture, home or auto maintenance, farm and equipment maintenance, automotive technology, metal fabrication, welding, graphic communications, architecture, construction, electronics, health occupations, child care, health care science, food science and nutrition, home economics, animal science, wildlife and recreation management, and gardening science. Many of these subjects can be learned with "hands-on" training in part-time jobs and volunteer programs unavailable to the public school student during the day.

If your child works at a part-time job during the high school years, give her credit for apprenticeship. We generally gave one credit per semester for ten to fifteen hours of work per week. Use your own judgment.

Teaching vocational courses involves creativity on your part. You can contact a vocational college and ask if it offers courses for the homeschooler or purchase vocational textbooks from it. You can suggest your child seek a part-time job related to the vocational choice. For instance, the child interested in fashion design or merchandising could work part-time in the retail clothing business. A student interested in marketing could seek an internship at an advertising agency.

Look around your area and expand your knowledge. A course doesn't have to come from a textbook. Learning by doing is attractive to many high school students.

Auto Technician by Choice

Our older son had had a hobby of taking things apart to see how they operated since he was old enough to use a screwdriver. As the years progressed, so did the size of his curiosity. He wanted to learn more about auto mechanics, something neither of us were even remotely versed in teaching.

We had an uncle, a retired electrical engineer, who had worked for General Motors. During a holiday we sent our son up to his uncle for a course in automotive technology. They spent three solid weeks together talking, working, and learning different things about automobiles. That course led to our son taking many courses at the local vocational college. Those vocational courses led to a master certification in automobile technology. Ultimately, that led to a wonderful career.

Our son boasts he's probably the only auto technician who can quote Shakespeare. He's also quick to remind us that he was correct, way back when, saying, "Explain to me how reading Shakespeare will help me get a job when I'm older." He was always too smart for his britches.

High School Coding

On some testing applications a code for the high school attended is required. What do I fill out as the code?

Have your high schooler fill out the testing application, not you. It's time he learns the bureaucracy of college life.

When he gets to the part that asks for the high school code, always leave it blank. Make sure to fill out the section directing where a copy of the test results should be sent with your home address. You won't be sending up any red flags by not filling in a high school code. Many homeschoolers take the SAT, entrance exams, placement tests, and scholarship applications and have the results sent to their homes.

Non-College-Bound Homeschooler

What options are available after graduation for the homeschooler who doesn't plan to attend college?

The same options are available for a homeschooler as for a public or private schooler who doesn't plan to attend college.

GREG HUGHES

Greg Hughes is completing his electrical apprenticeship program while working for an electrical contractor in West Virginia. Greg plans on going into partnership with his father, who is an established electrician.

When asked to comment on how homeschooling helped and hindered his life, Greg said, "Homeschooling didn't hinder my life at all. I wouldn't be who I am today, if I hadn't had the opportunity to homeschool. I have friends, young and old, and am much more open and outgoing because of the way I was raised and treated. Most parents, I think, raise children, and with some luck, they grow to be responsible adults. My parents didn't raise children, they raised young adults, and it certainly made a difference in my life."

Greg assures those who are contemplating homeschooling that, "Homeschooling isn't for everybody. You really have to love and be committed to your family. It wasn't all fun and games. We had our share of screaming matches, pouting for hours at the kitchen table over fractions and decimals, and I still dislike spelling. However, we were committed to making homeschooling work for our family. We have formed a closeness that many families don't have. I have the freedom to be who I am to the fullest."

There are vocational schools, the workforce, small businesses, and the military. You need to talk with your child and explore all the options.

Do homeschoolers have a difficult time entering vocational schools?

They don't appear to, as long as the parent has issued a diploma. Most vocational schools want to see a high school diploma or transcript. If the student doesn't have either, the vocational school will ask that the GED be taken before entrance is granted.

Most vocational schools are giving entrance exams to incoming students, measuring reading comprehension and mathematics skills. Make sure your child is prepared to take at least one or two entrance exams.

If my child doesn't plan to attend college, why prepare such a detailed course of study in high school?

We're sure you've heard the business world saying "Dress for Success." How about Learn for Success, or better yet, Homeschool for Success?

There are few high schoolers who know during their high school years what they want to pursue after graduation. Most students change their minds about their study options during the second year of college.

If you were given the chance to go back to college right now, would you choose a different career than the one you have presently? What does this suggest? Your child may decide to attend college or a vocational program later on after graduation from high school. Prepare him fully for that anticipated change of mind. Don't be lazy with the educational process based upon what your child states in his tenth grade year.

Our oldest wanted to be a pilot in ninth grade, a salesman in tenth grade, a physical therapist in eleventh grade, and a college professor in twelfth grade. He had completed one year in college as a psychology major before considering a change. Our youngest is one of the rare ones who has expressed an interest in the financial world since the beginning of seventh grade, and hasn't voiced any other option. Well, wait a minute; becoming a professional golfer would be his preference above all.

Teenagers Behind the Wheel

"Dad, can I borrow the car?"

What about driver's education?

In some states parents are permitted to teach their children driver's education whether they are homeschoolers or not. Call your local DPS (Department of Public Safety) for your particular state's requirements.

Athletic Opportunities for the High Schooler

Are athletic opportunities going to be available for my high school homeschooler?

Athletic opportunities are a big concern for the high schooler. This can be a determining factor for not homeschooling during the high school years, and we can certainly understand this concern. Just what sport options are available for the homeschooler and to what degree?

> **Parents are creating Web sites advertising their children's athletic abilities for scouts and coaches to view. You have to market your student's talents so they are noticed.**

If you live in a state that allows homeschoolers to participate in public school athletics, your athletic opportunities will be abundant. As we have mentioned in previous chapters, you're going to have to ask your homeschooling organizations, support groups, and other homeschoolers. There are plenty of homeschooling competitive teams playing across the country.

Athletic Scholarships

If a homeschooler displays an above-average talent in a sport, are college scouts ever going to get the chance to notice? Will athletic scholarships be available to the homeschooler? Are homeschoolers getting a chance to be competitive?

We wish we could say that an athletic homeschooler will get noticed by the scouts, but we would be wrong in assuming all homeschoolers are being given that chance. The fact is, if you homeschool your child you are the administration, teacher, and coach. So, part of your duty will be to "market" your own child. That's a tall order to fill. But it is the truth. Write or call the coach of the prospective college your child wishes to attend with a schedule of where and when your child will be playing. Ask that the coach come take a look at your child's abilities.

If your child possesses athletic talent, you already have placed him in many sport opportunities available in your area. Talent is talent. Scouts will find your child, hear about your child, read about your child, right? Maybe. If you don't live in a state that provides public school athletics to your homeschooler, you'll have to step in there and push.

Be aggressive. If your child is a super athlete, the scouts will find her, but you have to make her available to be found. Join everything having to do with the particular sport your child is interested in pursuing. Have the local newspapers cover your child's athletic progress, if possible. Most successful students who receive athletic scholarships probably had a parent helping with the process.

Homeschoolers Joining Public School Athletics

Will my high school homeschooler be able to join a public school athletic team?

Maybe, maybe not. Go to your public school system district office and ask. Not all states let homeschoolers join public school sports teams. It would be wonderful for homeschoolers if this were made available. After all, we pay school taxes, but don't benefit from them.

Another option would be to join a private school's athletic program. Call some of the private schools in your area. Many private schools are happy to extend athletic privileges to homeschoolers. You may have to have your student take one class with the school for this privilege. Perhaps this would be a good opportunity to study a foreign language.

Homeschooling Team Sports

Are team sports available within the homeschooling community?

Sports are available within the homeschooling community if, and only if, the homeschooling parents are willing to organize and facilitate the sports. You're the athletic department heads.

Check your local support group to see where your home-schoolers get together to play basketball, baseball, soccer, and other sports. You'll need to stay active in a support group or local homeschooling organization to be aware of all the sports opportunities. Since homeschoolers don't have a home-based gym, churches sometimes donate gyms once a week for that purpose. Call the churches in your area and ask what is available.

Put in Our Place

We would never have heard of the Christian Homeschool Association (CHSA) without the help of our support group. The CHSA in Pearland, Texas, organized a homeschool basketball league for girls and boys. We played private schools and other homeschool leagues. This was a fabulous network of parents donating time as coaches, trainers, scorekeepers, record keepers, concessionaires, and fund-raisers. The children worked hard and the parents worked even harder. We were very professional with our uniforms, gym bags, and letter jackets. Anything is available if the parent doesn't mind organizing or supporting the activity.

What about the cheerleaders?

When our sons played basketball we coached and sold concessions. Parents of children who want to be cheerleaders for the teams may be asked to teach cheers, sew uniforms, or drive them to the games. They're making it happen. There's no school administration to handle these requests. You're it.

However, we sure were put in our place the year our oldest son had basketball tryouts. The gym was filled with more than two hundred eager boys and girls. Standing next to us was a pretty young lady with her hair tied up with ribbons to match her shorts. We made the mistake of asking if she was trying out for cheer-leader. She politely informed us, "I want to play the sport, not cheer for it." We should have known better. Women are playing sports today, rather than watching from the sidelines. That bright young homeschooler put us in our place, big time.

High School Status Symbols

Can my homeschooler get a class ring or letter jacket?

What were the status symbols that you felt were most important during your high school years? The clothes you wore, the hairstyle you had, the car you drove? How about the class ring, letter jacket, or letter you earned? Those things are still important to some teenagers, even homeschoolers.

This was something that was important to our children when they entered their high school years. We remembered that it was just as important to us during our teenage years. Today you can have logos printed on bowling team shirts in less than a half hour. It wasn't hard to locate companies that sold class rings and jackets. It took longer to pick out the items we wanted than to find the companies that made them.

Ordering Class Rings and Letter Jackets

Class rings can be ordered from the jewelry counter of any Wal-Mart. They range in price from $70 to $500, depending on how fancy they are. The rings can be personalized with names, colors, clubs, and hobbies. Lord's Fine Jewelry, at P.O. Box 486, Piedmont, OK 73078-0486, (405) 373-2877, offers class rings for homeschoolers.

Letter jackets can be ordered from any company that personalizes T-shirts, hats, jackets, or gym bags. We contacted the Girl Scouts in our area for a list of distributors they recommended. The Girl Scouts put us in touch with several companies that provided this service. We even had T-shirts and gym bags made. Discounts are harder to obtain when purchasing only one or two jackets at a time, however. They ranged in price from $100 to $300.

Of course, the letters for the jackets have to be earned. The CHSA that sponsored our children's basketball league kept records of team members who earned their school letters. The parents and coaches arranged for the letters to be ordered and presented to the players at our awards banquet at the end of the year.

College Courses in High School

Can a high school homeschooler take college courses to supplement high school credits?

Yes. Several high schoolers in our support group enrolled at the community colleges for supplemental courses. Some classes can be for dual credit. This means the student receives a credit from you toward her high school diploma, and at the same time, the college gives her credit toward her college degree.

Some of the community colleges do not offer college credits to homeschoolers until they have taken the entrance exam, and there is a catch. Some colleges don't permit a student to take an entrance exam without a high school diploma or an SAT. Call your local college and ask what courses are available for the high school homeschooler. It will be happy to send you a catalogue or set up an interview with a counselor.

College Preparation

My high school homeschooler wants to go to college. How should we be preparing academically?

When your high schooler begins the ninth grade you need to sit down and help him map out a course chart for the next four years. We have included a sample in the back of this book. Call the universities that interest your child for their lists of required courses for high schoolers.

Most colleges request that incoming students have at least three years of a foreign language. You'll need to decide whether you'll teach the foreign language or hire a tutor.

Focus on reading comprehension, high-level vocabulary, writing, and solid mathematics courses. We also suggest that you teach your high schooler how to take notes, something a homeschooler seldom has to do. To make a smooth transition into college, a student needs encouragement and thorough reading skills.

Writing in High School

Should my high schooler take a writing course?

Even the colleges are realizing that not all college freshmen have college-level writing abilities. Your high schooler will have to take a writing test along with an English and mathematics entrance exam to see if remedial courses are needed. Remedial courses must be taken before beginning credit courses, and the college charges a fee for each remedial course taken.

The only way your high schooler is going to become a better writer is to write every day. Set up the computer and give him a topic to write about every day. Yes, every day! He needs to express his ideas on paper in a constructive, thought-provoking way. If you don't have a computer, a pen and pad of paper will work just as well. Set the timer and have him write for at least thirty minutes each day in addition to the writing research he should be doing. To do well on essays, reports, and term papers your high schooler should have at least one writing course.

Are there any Web sites to help with college preparation?

Web sites are created and deleted daily. We found the following Web sites:

GoCollege, http://www.gocollege.com

Financial Aid Information, http://www.finaid.org

College Board Online, http://www.collegeboard.org

College Edge, http://www.CollegeEdge.com

A Reading Course for the High Schooler

Nobody can tell you that your children must read everything from Dickens to Tolstoy, but we would like to suggest they read at least a few classics a year. Why? If they can read and understand the famous works of literature, they'll be able to zip through higher-level textbooks with ease.

We bought two identical books of each classic our children wanted to read. Then we sat across from them and each read a page aloud until we finished the book. We stopped and discussed things they didn't understand. Their reading skills increased dramatically from having to sound out harder words and comprehend tougher writing.

Most of the classics can be purchased for little money at library book sales, garage sales, thrift shops, and used bookstores. If you don't have access to a bookstore or are trying to cut costs, check out two of the same book at your library. A homeschooler can't live without the library.

I'll never get my high schooler to read the classics. Are comic books okay?

Never say never. You'll constantly be surprised at what your child will accomplish through homeschooling. Someone who was considering homeschooling informed us his child wouldn't read anything but comic books and that there are literature-based comic books. That might be true, but we've never seen them.

Don't hand your student a book and tell her to go read if she doesn't have good reading skills. That doesn't work unless you have a child who loves to read. Read aloud with your child. A seventeen-year-old will benefit just as much as a seven-year-old. We let our children read comic books all the time, but not during school time. Comic books were for recreation. Don't completely rule out some of the best literature available.

Should I have my high schooler read the books that are required reading for public school students?

LESHAY WRIGHT

LeShay Wright was homeschooled from kindergarten through her high school graduation, which was at the young age of fourteen. LeShay's parents made the choice to homeschool when their kind, sweet little girl became a student who ended up in the principal's office for shoving others. LeShay says that her mother, Kym, dove into homeschooling during a time when few support groups were available. Kym founded the "Preschool Park Days," where children could play with other homeschooled children and mothers could encourage one another with their endeavors.

LeShay points out that a definite benefit of homeschooling, besides having a wonderful relationship with her mother, is being able to tailor the education to the child. In LeShay's case, at the age of four she voiced an interest in veterinary medicine. Her parents designed an in-depth biology course with labs.

"Living on a farm gave us the ability to dissect anything and everything we could get, including rabbits, fetal pigs, sheep organs, a rattlesnake that became dinner, and even the bull when we had him butchered." She continues, "Homeschooling helped me by providing me with extensive studies in the areas that interested me and gave me the freedom to excel beyond assigned grade levels."

Because of LeShay's commitment to homeschooling, she graduated from high school at the age of fourteen. Her dad, not quite ready for his daughter to begin college, suggested she help her mother write a study unit on farm animals. Much research, two units, and one year later, she began college. Today, this seventeen-year-old veterinarian assistant/technician with forty-five college credits thanks her dedicated mother for teaching her how to study and prioritize tasks. LeShay lives by her mother's philosophy: Like the plants in a greenhouse, children should be nurtured until they can withstand the winds.

We took a look at some of the required reading for public school students. It included titles such as *Hiroshima,* by John Hersey; *Death Be Not Proud,* by John Gunther; *A Separate Peace,* by John Knowles; *The Light In the Forest,* by Conrad Richter; and *Fahrenheit 451,* by Ray Bradbury, to name a few. They were on the book list for our high school years, too, might we add, a long time ago. Use your judgment on what books to include as part of your children's high school reading assignments.

Homeschoolers don't have dictated reading lists. Create your own book list based on what you want your child to read. Just because the public schools recommend a book doesn't mean you have to choose the same.

Call the college your child plans to attend and ask what it suggests a high school student should have read before entering college. We did this for our first son. He read most of the required books and some of the required college selections before he began his college freshman year. In his opinion, it gave him a jump on his college work.

Shakespeare for the High Schooler

If you decide to incorporate Shakespeare in your high schooler's reading list, you may want to purchase the *Barron's Shakespeare Made Easy* publications. These are wonderful for easy comprehension. They are modern English versions side-by-side with the full original text.

Reading some of the classics can be boring and tedious, especially for those students who don't enjoy reading. It really is up to the individual family. Some homeschoolers read nothing but the classics. Some read a few classics mixed in with recently written novels. Some choose short stories of famous literature.

Despite the fact that our sons placed *Romeo and Juliet* and *Jane Eyre* in the category of "chick flicks," they did read each one. About the only two books that our children absolutely gave a "thumbs down" were *Moby Dick* and *The House of the Seven Gables.* We have to agree those weren't good choices on our part.

> To read Shakespeare or not to read Shakespeare, that is the question.

We let our sons provide a list of their favorites for you:

The Old Man and the Sea, by Ernest Hemingway

Dracula, by Bram Stoker

Night, by Elie Wiesel

Twenty Thousand Leagues under the Sea, by Jules Verne

Journey to the Center of the Earth, by Jules Verne

The Time Machine, by H. G. Wells

Treasure Island, by Robert Louis Stevenson

Hamlet, by William Shakespeare

Where the Red Fern Grows, by Wilson Rawls

The Pearl, by John Steinbeck

Quoth the Raven, Nevermore!

Does my high schooler need to have a poetry course?

That's about the same as asking, "Does my high schooler need to have a geometry course, or a biology course, or a Latin course?" The answer is that what your high schooler needs or doesn't need is totally up to what you want her to experience. In our case, a well-rounded education was what we were pursuing, and poetry was part of the experience.

Reading poetry helps us to understand the treasures of another person's soul or to see life from a different perspective. Poetry enhances reading comprehension, plain and simple. Students today are reciting poetry far more often than they would care to admit when they learn rap music.

Browse through the poetry section of a bookstore. Enter your child's poetry in a contest. *Writer's Magazine,* which comes out monthly, advertises poetry contests for students. Here are some Web sites for poetry:

http://www.poets.org

http://www.sympatico.ca/ray.saitz/poetunit.txt

http://www.sympatico.ca/ray.saitz/arrow.txt

From High School to the SAT to College

The Scholastic Assessment Test, not to be confused with the Stanford Achievement Test, is used by most colleges as an entrance exam. There are many schools of thought about this test, one being that it's a test to determine how well the student tests. Nevertheless, it's still required of most students entering college. Homeschoolers must score well, if not better than average, to be accepted into some colleges that have different standards for homeschoolers than for public or private school students.

Homeschoolers, if they have had a well-rounded course of study, do well on their SAT tests, but it doesn't happen just because they've homeschooled. It's a must that your homeschooler familiarize herself with at least a few practice tests before taking the actual one.

Barron's SAT Practice Tests and *Princeton Review* are books that help the student study for the test. We purchased several of these practice tests and helpful hints a full year before our son took his test. The books contained excellent vocabulary lists that we incorporated into our child's language course.

Although the SAT is not a measurement of the student's abilities, it is an important step in making the transition from high school to college as smooth as possible. Make sure you have taught your child algebra and geometry reasoning skills for the math section of the SAT. For the language section of the SAT, students will be required to comprehend what they read and to have an excellent vocabulary. If we had it to do over again, we would have introduced the SAT vocabulary words beginning in the eighth grade.

The Perfect Score

Some colleges want to see a 1200 or better on the SAT from a homeschooler. Then again, they want to see that from a public school student, too. Community colleges are more lenient about

SAT scores. The SAT is still a valued asset when applying for college entrance. Your student will only do as well as he has prepared. It's just not true that a homeschooler will naturally score higher than a public or private school student without reading, language, basic algebra, and geometry preparation. Those who have prepared for the SAT do well. Those who have not score low.

We Want Homeschoolers, We Want Homeschoolers!

I've heard that colleges are begging for homeschoolers. Is that true?

We have found no evidence of that. Colleges are businesses, and like any business, they are recruiting students who have the skills and financial means to attend. If homeschoolers have the appropriate SAT score and the financial means, they pretty much will have an easy time of being accepted to most colleges in the United States.

As for the rumor that homeschoolers are better students in college, there are no surveys to document that as yet. Maybe we can boast that homeschoolers have excellent reading and study skills, but that's too general a statement to be a fact. We can state that homeschoolers are not being turned away from colleges for having been homeschooled.

Are colleges recruiting homeschoolers for scholarship opportunities?

It doesn't appear that scholarship money is being given just because the student was homeschooled. Colleges recruit certain students (usually gifted athletes and strong academic scholars), but so far, not students who were homeschooled exclusively.

What documents are requested of a homeschooler when applying to college?

Your high school student will need one or all of the following: a transcript, diploma or GED certificate, SAT/ACT scores, and possibly an entrance exam so she will be excluded from remedial classes.

Homeschooling and the Military

Are homeschoolers accepted into the military?

With the vast amount of military families homeschooling their own children on and off base, we would venture to say they would never do anything to jeopardize their own children's potential military careers. Years ago homeschoolers had a tough time entering the military without a high school diploma or at least a GED, and that seems to stand true today. The good news is that a homeschool diploma is just as valid as a public or private school diploma.

Upon entering the military your high schooler will be asked to take an entrance exam, similar to the remedial exclusion exam given by most colleges. This test is given to all entering military personnel, not just homeschoolers. Call your local military office and inquire about the current enrollment opportunities for your homeschooled child.

Naming Your School

Should I name our homeschool?

It isn't necessary, but some families choose to name their homeschools. Why? When your child fills out a job application he'll be asked to supply the name of the last school attended. Rather than having to explain on a job application that he was homeschooled, therefore there is no school name, it is easier to state the name of your individual homeschool. The same is true for driver's permit, college placement test, and health insurance forms.

On the other hand, some families name their schools just because they're proud of who they are. Many families have T-shirts and hats printed up displaying their school names for wearing on field trips. We found that at special homeschooling events many families even had created logos to go with their school names.

Homeschoolers and the GED

The GED, or General Educational Development test, is a test to qualify for a high school equivalency diploma. There are five parts to the test: writing, literature, social studies, math, and science. The tests are the same nationwide, but each state sets its own rules for who is eligible to take the tests as well as the minimum score to pass.

Should I have my high schooler take the GED?

We are firm believers that a homeschooled child who is issued a graduation diploma need not take the GED. Check your state's laws for what is required. If your child is required to take a GED to enter college, think of it as an entrance exam. In some states your high schooler must be age eighteen to take the GED. Call your nearest community college for information on when and where the GED test is given. There are also a few books that assist the homeschooler with studying for the GED:

Barron's How to Prepare for the GED, by Barron's

Cliffs Studyware for the GED, book and CD-ROM, by
Cliff Notes

Testing Out—Credit for College Classes

What is the CLEP test?

CLEP stands for College-Level Examination Program tests. College credit may be earned by taking a CLEP test in general college math, calculus with elementary functions, college algebra, college algebra/trigonometry, and trigonometry, as well as a variety of other courses. For information on CLEP testing, contact this organization:

> Tour a college campus with your high schooler when she is in tenth or eleventh grade.

CLEP, Box 6601, Princeton, NJ
08541, (609) 771-7865,
e-mail: clep@ets.org

How can I find where the test sites are located for the CLEP tests?

The general information contact for a list of test sites is:

College Board, 45 Columbus Ave., New York, NY 10023,
(212) 713-8000, http://www.collegeboard.org

Academic Scholarship Programs

Are academic scholarships available to the homeschooler?

Academic scholarships are just as available to the homeschooler as they are to the public/private schooled student. Make sure your high schooler takes the PSAT, which is the practice test for the SAT. This test will place your child in the eligibility range for academic scholarships. In the meantime, have her contact the college of her choice and speak with a counselor about available scholarships. Give her the power of independence by letting her ask questions on her own. You are preparing her for college.

If you are looking for an organization that readily supplies financial scholarship programs just for homeschoolers to come knocking on your door, you may be looking for a long time. Start to inquire about scholarships in your child's tenth and eleventh grade levels. Call every organization you can think of that might offer essay contests or scholarship outreach programs, such as

> **Teach them. Help them. Let them grow up.**

charity organizations, men's and women's organizations, foreign language clubs, businesses, chambers, agriculture associations, and so on. Here are a few:

Financial Aid Information, http://www.finaid.org

KapLoan: Student Loan Information Program, http://www.kaploan.com

Scholarship Search, http://www.collegeboard.org/ fundfinder/bin/fundfind01.pl

Too Young to Graduate

What happens when a homeschooler finishes his high school courses before he turns eighteen? This became a concern of our family when our sixteen-year-old was ready to graduate. He had progressed so quickly. We felt we had gone too fast, pushed way too hard, demanded more than necessary at his age. Nevertheless, we had moved at his required pace. He wanted to learn. We taught. In our opinion, he was ready for college academically, but not emotionally. We faced the real dilemma of what to do with this child/adult.

We considered correspondence courses, enrolling at the community college or vocational school, repeating courses for added academic strength, letting him work more hours, or creating a home business. We were avoiding the inevitable: letting him grow up.

Although each student adjusts to college, a job, or a vocational program at a different rate, they all still need to be given the opportunity to try one, even if they're only sixteen years old. By the time you reach the graduation stage, you'll know your student very well. You'll have developed wonderful communication skills, so take advantage of them. Talk and listen, but mostly listen to what he wants to do next. Don't be afraid of letting him move on, even though he may be younger than what society dictates as the norm. Homeschooling will afford your child opportunities beyond belief.

Letting Them Go

How will I know when it's time for my high schooler to graduate?

This seems like such an easy question to answer for non-homeschoolers. If your child were in the public school system, she would simply graduate when the senior year was over, whether the textbooks were finished or the skills needed to move on were learned. You, on the other hand, will need to decide what you want your child to accomplish before graduating. The following were our graduation requirements:

- Finish all senior level textbooks, supplements, writing projects, and reading list.

- Have driver's license and knowledge of life lessons mentioned in chapter 3.

- Have taken the SAT/ACT and applied to college.

Is there a final plan, form, or document that must be filed upon my high schooler's graduation?

Verify your state's homeschooling laws for graduation requirements. Your child may need to be tested before the diploma is issued. If you're in a state where you issue the diploma, transcript, or whatever else you deem necessary, chances are there won't be a school district or state organization to notify. For sure there's no national organization that must be notified. In most cases there is no form or document to be filed. All that remains is to give your child his diploma and have the graduation party.

If you are working with a correspondence or umbrella school, check to see what its plan of graduation is. It may issue the diploma based on successful test results.

What happens when my child is finished learning all his courses? Is that it?

You create a transcript and issue a diploma. Then you sit back and breathe a sigh of relief. The job of being your children's educator ends. Your job as their parent goes on forever, but in a whole different way. You now get to watch them grow and succeed as adults. Don't worry, you'll have prepared them well. Someday it will be their job to homeschool their own children. Pat yourself on the back, and take a vacation to some exotic place—without the children. You'll deserve it.

The High School Diploma

Plan to issue a diploma and transcript to your homeschool graduate. It makes life easier for the homeschooler planning to attend college or enroll in the military. If you have the benefit of working under an umbrella plan, correspondence school, comprehensive curriculum course, or state-regulated issuance, your job will be easy. After your child passes the high school exit exam, the diploma and transcript possibly will be provided.

Diplomas can be self-designed or special-ordered. Parents designing a diploma are often confused about what to print on the diploma. Do you call it a "Homeschooled Diploma," "Tom's Graduation Diploma," "Mom and Dad's Finished Diploma," "Yeah, I Did It Diploma," or what? Parents are uncomfortable with naming "where" their children graduated. Just call it a "High School Diploma." Date and sign it with your name. You need not name your homeschool unless you want to do so.

Necessity or Not?

Although not every homeschooling family feels the necessity for issuing a diploma, it was very important to us. Every senior looks forward to graduation day. Some of the support groups get together to host graduation ceremonies, with fathers passing out diplomas and mothers breathing a sigh of great accomplishment. Maybe parents of homeschoolers should receive a diploma as well. We certainly received our education all over again.

Decide upon a date for graduation. A homeschooler can graduate anytime. We graduated our oldest in the month of December. He enrolled in college in January. Sometimes it's easier to enter your child in college during a winter semester when it is less crowded.

You might want to order two copies of a diploma, one for your child, one for the file. There are two companies that provide quality work in producing personalized homeschool documents such as stationery, report cards, transcripts, and personalized diplomas with your school name and choice of logos:

Graduation, Inc., P.O. Box 59627, Dallas, TX 75229-1876, (214) 258-5723, e-mail: homeschol@gte.net

Educational Support Foundation, 1523 Moritz, Houston, TX 77055, (713) 870-9194

Transcript Anxiety

It's natural to experience some anxiety when preparing the transcript. It need not be a fear-provoking event. You may use the copy of our transcript in the back of this book or design your own.

We kept careful records and created a transcript based on the yearly report cards. Credits are issued upon completion of each course and recorded. Use your best judgment on the number of credits issued.

Parents want to know whether colleges have ever refused a parent-designed transcript. We didn't have any problems, and none of our homeschooling friends experienced difficulties. Be smart and don't design a transcript on heart-shaped pink paper. Use only high-grade white paper.

When recording the transcript data, determine what type of courses your child has studied. If your child took regular classes, then A's are worth 4 points, B's are worth 3 points, C's are worth 2 points, D's are worth 1 point, and F's receive no points. It is up to the parent to call the state organization for the particulars on courses and earned credits necessary for graduation.

Figuring Grade Point Averages

What's to stop a parent from placing all A's on a high school transcript?

What's to stop you from giving your child all A's? Quite frankly, nothing. As a matter of fact, why wouldn't a homeschooler maintain a 4.0 grade average? If you never move on until a lesson has been learned and retained, naturally your student will be doing A work.

Homeschooling affords the opportunity to spend as much time as needed for your child to comprehend thoroughly every lesson taught, *before* moving to the next lesson or course. If you are skimming through the educational process, your child is the one who suffers in the long run, missing the basic fundamentals. Promise yourself to go slowly, teach thoroughly, and finish each course. Then go ahead and give your child that 4.0 grade point average. If you have done your job properly, he will pass the entrance exam for college with ease.

The Homeschooled Graduate

So what happens to a homeschooler who has graduated?

She has the same advantages that are available to all high school graduates. Whether it is college, vocational school, the workforce, or the military, she begins adult life equipped with the education you have provided.

What happens to the parents who have homeschooled their child when the job is complete?

You'll experience some days of loneliness and emptiness, but then again you may jump for joy with all the free time you have. Best of all, you'll feel a sense of accomplishment.

Having gone through your high school education again, don't rule out taking the college entrance exam yourself and starting a new career. You'll be surprised at how well your child prepared you, too.

In Summary

Ah, yes, the high school years. They are certainly a time of growing and learning in a young adult's life. Well, at best, it's definitely
a challenge getting through the teenage years. Homeschooling
conclusively eliminates some of the stress associated with those
years for your child and for you.

It's a commitment on your part. But it's certainly worth it
when you hand your young adult that diploma and receive a
heartfelt thank-you. It's sure to provoke some tears, too. Enjoy the
supplement chapter next.

CHAPTER 9

Creating Supplements for Your Child

Beware of the Conceited Homeschooling Parent

Something happened while homeschooling our children that we never expected. We discovered we were pretty good at this teaching thing. As a matter of fact, we were downright fantastic at motivating our children to learn. So good were we that the textbooks weren't enough to satisfy our children's curiosity in the science and social studies courses. So, while we were patting ourselves on the back, we never realized we were about to create more work for ourselves by researching educational supplements for our boys. Beware of the conceited homeschooling parent. We were big-time homeschoolers.

Homeschooling was benefiting our children's needs and consuming every bit of our free time. Not only could we say we were teachers, we were also writers and designers of personalized curricula. It didn't take long before other homeschooling families were asking us to design personalized courses for their children. What had we gotten ourselves into?

The Supplement

What is a supplement?

A supplement is any additional educational information above and beyond the textbook curriculum you want your child to learn. Supplements are meant to enhance the textbook curriculum that your child is studying.

> In the public school system our children considered learning to be a chore. Homeschooling made learning a hands-on, fun experience.

Are supplements necessary?

Prior to beginning the homeschooling process our children never wanted to do anything extra that had to do with school. Homeschooling changed all that.

We noticed how our children enjoyed watching the Discovery Channel. They didn't feel that they were doing schoolwork when they were watching videos that interested them. We didn't give them a test or require them to write a summary after each video. We discussed what they learned over dinner that evening.

> Spend an entire day or even an entire week watching educational videos with your child. It'll be a memorable homeschooling experience, popcorn and all.

We got to thinking, if they got excited about watching videos about their favorite topics, they might be just as eager to select topics of interest to study. So, we put the question to them, "If you could choose a topic to study in depth, what would it be?" One son said, "Egyptian times, or maybe castles, knights, and dragons." The other said, "Sharks, everything about sharks."

SHARNESSA SHELTON

The American public is going to hear quite a bit about Sharnessa Shelton in the years to come. This homeschool graduate is one of the two lead singers in the Christian pop band V*Enna. (Visit V*Enna's Web site at http://www.V-enna.com.) Her record contract is with the Christian record company Essential, in Nashville, Tennessee. Sharnessa attended the School of Creative Ministries under the International Bible Institute of London, where she was offered an audition for the pop band, which is based in Manchester, England.

Sharnessa took time out of her hectic schedule to share her feelings about homeschooling. She beams when she declares, "The benefits of homeschooling are endless! The one-on-one is invaluable. I so enjoyed being able to pursue my delights and subjects I really enjoyed learning about. I loved that we were able to do classes in such creative ways, with museums, courses, seminars, videos, hands-on ways, community concerts, field trips. I love the fact that in homeschooling the love of learning isn't squelched, but instead just flourishes. I suppose, in some cases, though certainly not ours, a negative would be when parents bring the classroom into the home, just wanting to do 'school at home' as opposed to getting to truly enjoy the freedom that homeschooling can offer. It was an amazing experience. I will forever be grateful to my parents who gave so much, but who I know also gained immensely from it. My husband-to-be and I are going to one day homeschool our kids, too."

They Asked, We Provided

Castles, knights, dragons, sharks; we had our hot topics to create supplements. They asked, and we provided.

The research began, with the boys eagerly peeking into our notes each day. It finally dawned on us to involve them in the process. By doing so, they developed excellent researching techniques.

Do all homeschoolers prepare supplements?

No. Some parents teach straight from a textbook-driven curriculum, and that's quite sufficient. This chapter is devoted to the extra things that make homeschooling attractive for so many families.

Nobody says you have to provide supplements for your child. It doesn't mean you're lazy if you don't. The necessary course work can be enough of a load to carry.

> Homeschooling is an individual preference in the way information is taught and learned.

Do Not Compare Homeschooling Families

"Did you hear that the Jones family is memorizing *War and Peace*?"

"Well, I heard that the Edwards family is able to speak and write five languages."

"That's nothing. The Hudson children are reading at their appropriate grade levels."

How will I compare to other homeschooling parents?

It's good for homeschooling families to share ideas, especially when looking for new and fresh motivational techniques. Homeschooling is an individual preference in the way information is taught and learned. Never compare and criticize one homeschooling family's techniques against another. You'll do what's right for your family.

> Spend an entire day playing Scrabble as a spelling lesson. Challenge each word, and make children use their dictionaries.

Are All Supplements Alike?

Do supplements have to be in written form?

Nothing says you must have a supplement presented in written form. Each time you practice flash cards with your child, play a board game, or put a puzzle together, you are using a supplement. When you're in the car pointing out road signs or directions, you are creating a supplement. Teaching your child to help with the laundry, count money, and train the dog are supplements. Supplements can be as intensive as you desire or as light as you want. It's your call.

> Supplements find you.
> You don't find supplements.

How About Next Year?

Can I wait until I'm more comfortable with the whole homeschooling thing before using a supplement?

Of course you can wait until you are more comfortable with homeschooling. However, if you're trying to think of a possible supplement for your child, don't. Supplements just happen. They happen when your child has an interest in a subject that isn't covered well enough with the textbook to meet their needs. Supplements find you; you don't find them.

Could I work with another homeschooling parent to create a supplement that both our families would enjoy?

Yes, two heads are better than one. The ideas will be endless. The social interaction between your children and the other family will be beneficial. Face it, sometimes children learn better in groups. That doesn't mean everything has to be taught or learned with the competitiveness of a group, just that sometimes supplements work better with many children expressing opinions, questions, and eagerness to learn.

> **Sit beside your high schooler and tour the Internet as a supplement.**

Our support group moms prepared a science supplement that involved studying rockets, NASA, and the space program. We organized a rocket launching day that was a big success with the homeschooling fathers.

Preparing a supplement with other homeschooling families is obviously less time consuming in the research department. Plus, the children enjoy getting together.

The Internet as a Supplement

Could my child and I explore what's available on the Internet as a supplement?

That would be an excellent way to see what subjects interest your child. We encourage this for all ages. Make sure you and your children do this together so you can provoke conversation about subjects they find interesting. You must lead this type of education. Don't let them just play on the computer with no guidance. Remind yourself that homeschooling is educating your child. The Internet can become nothing but a browser for commercials if your child doesn't know where to look for information.

Field Trips Are the Best Supplements

Are field trips considered supplements?

Yes. Visit the zoo, take an animal observation class together, tour a fire station, and see a museum. Have a high schooler visit different places of employment. Explore the stars with a telescope. Go camping in the desert.

Time: Something You Might Not Have

Creating written supplements takes time, something you'll have less and less of as you pursue homeschooling. You might try leaving one day a week for supplements only. We found the other four days were more than enough time to cover the state requirements. Try some of these tips:

- Prepare written or intensive supplements during the summer months or holiday breaks.

- Ask an interested relative to prepare a supplement for your child. It will give your child a different perspective on teaching styles.

- Involve your children in the research process. Have them select books, games, puzzles, and helpful resource materials.

- Keep supplements simple and fun. Save the intensive supplements for the high school student learning to write a term paper.

- Form a homeschool reading group with other homeschooling families. Select a book for the group to read and review.

- Read the newspaper together.

- Teach a middle schooler how to follow the stock market.

- Allow your high schooler to take a college course.

- Visit a nursing home and have your child give an oral book report or read to the residents.

> Cutting out paper doll outfits with scissors is a fun supplement for an elementary-age homeschooler. Search for the historic paper dolls sold in most major bookstores.

- Get to know another homeschooling family and switch children for the day.

- Learn a foreign language while in the car together traveling to all those extracurricular activities.

Why do I need supplements?

Supplements simply are more fun than textbook learning every day. Supplements aid parents in defining their own teaching methods, rather than emulating the public school techniques.

AMBER HEINTZBERGER

"Homeschooling gave me the sense that I am my own person and don't have to follow strict guidelines set by society for how people should live their lives. There are so many things available to home-schoolers, and students should get involved in everything they can. It was through homeschooling groups that I was able to participate in science fairs and reading groups, and meet other kids dealing with issues similar to what I was facing."

Amber Heintzberger's parents chose homeschooling as a more effective and open means of schooling for their daughter, who was academically advanced, but unhappy with the academic and social situation at the school she attended. At age seventeen Amber received her A.A. in liberal arts from Isothermal Community College and at twenty-one her B.A. from Wofford College; she was on the dean's list at both colleges, was in *Who's Who Among Students in American Junior Colleges,* and was a member of Phi Theta Kappa Honor Society. She also spent a summer attending the University of Bath in England. In athletics she lettered in track and field and fencing.

An avid horsewoman, Amber teaches young children to ride. She achieved the H-A level rating in the U.S. Pony Club. Her involvement in equestrian events opened the door to a career in horse-related journalism, and directly out of college she began writing for *The Chronicle of the Horse* and other publications. In 1999, Amber traveled twice to Germany to cover international competitions.

Amber's interest in travel has led her on study and research trips all over the world. Today she works in procurement at BMW Manufacturing Corp. While experiencing the corporate world and learning to speak German, Amber continues writing and broadening her journalistic horizons.

Let's suppose your middle school child is learning to memorize the list of presidents of the United States and you're discussing the differences between the Democratic and Republican Parties. Your child is nodding her head in what appears to be understanding, but you know very well she hasn't the slightest idea what you're talking about.

This is the time to introduce a supplement on the political parties and their philosophies. Maybe you have a clear picture of the differences of each party, but you can be sure that a seventh grader doesn't have a clue. Here's your chance to research and present a supplement that explains the political parties in the language that your seventh grader can digest.

Specializing an Education

Perhaps you have a student who is interested in studying the law. You're listening to your child read from his government textbook how the Supreme Court is often asked to decide important legal issues, when your child asks, "Like what type of important issues, Dad?"

This is your chance to answer, "Cases like *Brown v. Board of Education of Topeka* (1954). The Court held laws enforcing segregated schools to be unconstitutional and it called for desegregation of schools with all deliberate speed. Or how about *Mapp v. Ohio* (1961) when the Court extended the federal exclusionary rule to the states, preventing prosecutors from using illegally obtained evidence in a criminal trial. Or *Miranda v. Arizona* (1966), in which the Court declared that before questioning suspects, police must inform them of their right to remain silent, that any statements they make can be used against them, and that they have the right to remain silent until they have an attorney, which the state will provide if they cannot afford to pay."

Can you tell we prepared a legal supplement for our high schooler? When first asked the question above, we responded with the standard "I don't know, son." We weren't able to rattle off the cases listed above, but ask us now, or ask our children.

The Inquisitive Middle Schooler

Your brilliant sixth grader asks how she can get information on the laws that seem outdated but are still kept on the books of several states. Don't you wish you could rattle off the following list to her?

In Lexington, Kentucky, it is illegal to carry an ice-cream cone in your pocket.

In Alabama, you can't call someone a skunk without risking arrest.

In Hartford, Connecticut, you can't cross a street while walking on your hands.

In Portland, Oregon, you can't roller-skate into a public rest room.

In Denver, Colorado, you can't bicycle with your feet higher than the front of your bike.

In New York City, bean shooters are illegal weapons for children.

In Winnetka, Illinois, you can be arrested if you take off your shoes in a movie theater and your feet stink.

Play Trivial Pursuit as a supplement.

Trivia can be a wonderful supplement for the curious homeschooler. Playing the game of Trivial Pursuit may be all your child needs for just such a supplement. Plan a day of doing nothing but that for school.

Researching Topics

Enthusiasm over creating written supplements isn't automatic, especially when you have a million things you need to do around the house. Sometimes researching doesn't come easily, but the good news is that you can develop quick and efficient ways to make it less time consuming.

It's been a long time since I had to research.
I need a refresher course on what's available.

Every library has a reference section. Reference material includes but is not limited to encyclopedias, dictionaries, biographical works, atlases, almanacs, books of quotations, magazines, newspapers, microfilm, and of course, the Internet.

> **Learning to read a map is a wonderful supplement for a teen who is learning to drive.**

If there is one concept that colleges assume, it's that all students have learned to research a topic. Unfortunately, most high school and middle school students are never taught the proper way to do research. Finding information is difficult if you have poor researching skills. Once your child learns these skills, he'll experience less intimidation in the library. Learning to do research at a young age is a powerful asset for the college-bound student.

Power Shortage

If you or your child walked into a library and the computers were down, would you know where to look for the books that you needed, or would you go home? Just such a thing happened to us on one trip to the library. Our children announced, "Oh, well, we can't find the books we want now." We

> **Word searches, hidden pictures, mazes, and crossword puzzles make excellent supplements.**

couldn't believe our ears. They didn't have the slightest idea how to locate books without the computer database at their fingertips. Think about this for a moment. Would you be able to locate the books you needed?

Many libraries arrange nonfiction books according to the Dewey Decimal System of numbering to indicate the subject matter contained in each book. The Dewey Decimal System divides the fields of knowledge into the ten main categories listed below. It would be a good idea if you taught your child this system.

000–099   General works (reference material)

100–199	Philosophy
200–299	Religion
300–399	Social sciences (economics, law, government)
400–499	Language
500–599	Pure sciences
600–699	Technology (engineering, aviation, inventions)
700–799	The arts (architecture, music, sports)
800–899	Literature
900–999	History (includes geography, travel books, and biography)

Selecting the Subject

If you are preparing a supplement for a certain interest or course, you have already selected the subject. The subject should have chosen you, not the other way around. Listen to those questions from your child. Did your child ask you something but you didn't know the answer? If so, that was your selection.

It's important to select a topic that will hold your child's interest and that is prepared for her grade and age level. The idea is to make your child an authority on the subject that you have researched for her. Supplements should be fun for your child. Make them interesting, colorful, and full of activities and wonderful things to do.

Preparing a Written Supplement

Many parents feel they could never write a supplement, but you'd be surprised at your skills after you homeschool for a few months. You see, not only will your child be receiving an excellent education, but you'll be reinforcing your elementary, middle school, or even high school education, too. So, go ahead and write that supplement.

You're at a bit of a loss if you don't have word processing capabilities on your computer. If it's not a long supplement you can simply write it out and have a copy made for each of you to read and go over together. Attach directions for the activities that go along with the supplement. Use easy-to-read language written in proper English, but not in technical terms.

A Pro in No Time

Are you artistic? Now's your chance to write, draw, perform, design, paint, build, or do those talented things you do. Over the years, these are the supplements that found us.

- Our sons designed and built a life-size puppet theater that trifolded neatly to fit in our truck. We made puppets, wrote plays, and performed at the local library, at day-care centers, and for our support group.

- Our sons took the old lawn mower apart and built a go-cart. They developed a knowledge of proper tool usage. We taught driving safety and let them design obstacle courses to run.

- We studied a supplement on medieval times that included music of the period, children's games such as stilt-walking and juggling, and a "fit-for-a-king feast" our sons cooked and served for their friends, as well as making stained glass, pottery, and a model of a castle.

- Together, we planted an experimental garden using excessive amounts of chemicals to test the vegetables' toxicity levels.

- We created an ecosystem in a large fish tank that led to crickets escaping all over the house—obviously, not one of our favorites.

- Our oldest prepared for and entered an all-natural body-building contest. He took first place in the teen category and third in novice. This supplement complemented his biology course, helping him learn individual muscles and develop a nutrition plan.

- To prove a point in pattern and sequence development, the boys reluctantly learned tap dancing time steps. They weren't exactly Gregory Hines, but they had fun.

- We trained and entered our collie, Ariel, in a dog show. What a disaster. She just sat there breathing heavily, but it was good for a laugh.

- The boys took horseback riding lessons and learned to groom and care for a horse.

- When our oldest got his driver's permit, we drove across the country to the Grand Canyon, stopping along the way to visit any historic place upon which we came.

In Summary

Supplements aren't mandatory for homeschooling families. They do enhance textbook curricula and offer interesting information specialized for your child. Whether or not you create supplements is entirely up to you. Should you decide to research and write your own supplement, have fun. You should feel thoroughly educated by now in the world of homeschooling. Now, it's your turn to come up with supplements that interest your child. We've enjoyed sharing this aspect of homeschooling with you. The final chapter will give you samples of report cards, transcript information, lesson plan forms, and organizations available to homeschoolers.

CHAPTER 10

Organizations to Help Answer Your Questions

Helpful Organizations

One thing is certainly a fact of homeschooling: Change remains constant. So we dutifully apologize for any invalid organization addresses and phone numbers. Also, new homeschooling organizations are forming daily, and we apologize for those we didn't list.

We have included the federal government contacts because it is important that homeschoolers stay current with homeschooling laws, education laws, compulsory attendance laws, and other pertinent information that affects homeschooling rights in the United States. It is your duty as a homeschooler to stay informed about the regulations of the federal and state governments. There is no excuse for ignorance of the law.

Most homeschooling support groups assign the task of keeping up with the federal and state education laws to one or two members. These members report their findings weekly or monthly to the entire support group. It really is a good idea to join a support group even if only to keep abreast of the legal issues that homeschoolers face.

Federal Government Contacts

United States Capitol switchboard, (202) 224-3121

The Honorable [your senator's name], United States Senate, Washington, DC 20510, http://www.senate.gov

The Honorable [your representative's name], United States House of Representatives, Washington, DC 20515, http://www.house.gov

The Honorable [your governor's name], Governor of [your state], [Capital city, state name, and ZIP code]

Mr./Ms. Justice [last name], The Supreme Court, Washington, DC 20543

The President, The White House, Washington, DC 20500

The Vice President, The United States Senate, Washington, DC 20510

National Homeschool Organizations

Adventist Home Educator, P.O. Box 836, Camino, CA 95709-0836, (916) 647-2110, http://www.adventtech.com/ahe

Alliance for Parental Involvement in Education, P.O. Box 59, East Chatham, NY 12060-0059, (518) 392-6900, http://www.croton.com/allpie

Alternative Education Resource Organization, 417 Roslyn Road, Roslyn Heights, NY 11577, (516) 621-2195

American Homeschool Association, P.O. Box 3142, Palmer, AK 99645, http://www.home-ed-press.com/AHA/aha.html

Home School Legal Defense Association (HSLDA),
P.O. Box 3000, Purcellville, VA 20134, (540) 338-5600,
http://www.hslda.org

Jewish Home Educator's Network c/o Koenig, 409 North Broad,
Carlinville, IL 62626, http://www.snj.com/jhen

National Association for Mormon Home Educators,
2770 South 1000 West, Perry, UT 84302

National Association of Catholic Home Educators,
P.O. Box 787, Montrose, AL 36559, http://www.nache.com

National Handicapped Homeschoolers Association Network,
5383 Alpine Rd., SE, Oglalla, WA 98359, (206) 857-4257

National Home Education Research Institute (NHERI), 5000 Deer
Park Dr. SE., Salem, OR 97301-9392, (503) 581-8600

National Homeschool Association, P.O. Box 290, Hartland, MI
48353, (513) 772-9580, http://www.n-h-a.org

Native American Homeschool Association, P.O. Box 979, Fries,
VA 24330, (540) 744-3640, http://www.expage.
com/page/nahomeschool

Informational Radio Stations

Home Education Radio Network, P.O. Box 3338, Idaho Springs,
CO 80452, (303) 567-4092

Home School Legal Defense Association, P.O. Box 3000, Purcellville, VA 20134 (540) 338-5600. Offers a syndicated radio
show, *Home School Heartbeat*, a daily two-minute show
broadcast on over 150 stations nationwide.

State Homeschool E-mail Contacts

Alabama: hls@prodigy.net

Alaska: grallsup@alaskalife.net

Arizona: afhe@primenet.com/~afhe

Arkansas: fcouncil@alpha-net.net

California: cheaofca@aol.com

Colorado: office@chec.org

Connecticut: teach.info@pobox.com

Delaware: jcpoeii@juno.com

Florida: circle@ao.net

Georgia: ghea@mindspring.com

Hawaii: oamastpro@aol.com

Idaho: prche@ida.net

Illinois: ICHE83@juno.com

Indiana: iahe@inhomeeducators.org

Iowa: niche@netins.net

Kansas: BARFIELD@cjnetworks.com

Kentucky: chek@kvnet

Louisiana: Burg6@juno.com

Maine: homeschl@midcoast.com

Maryland: MACHE@juno.com

Massachusetts: Info@masshope.org

Michigan: inchmi@ibm.net

Minnesota: mache@isd.net

Mississippi: MHEA@juno.com

Missouri: match@christianmail.net

Montana: white@gomontana.com

Nebraska: nchea@navix.net

Nevada: linkedhearts@hotmail.com

New Hampshire: parison@chenh.mv.com

New Jersey: enochnji@uscom.com

New Mexico: cape-nm@juno.com

New York: Info@leah.org

North Carolina: nche@mindspring.com

North Dakota: ndhsa@wdata.com

Ohio: cheohome@bright.net

Oklahoma: chefofok@aol.com

Oregon: oceanet@oceanetwork.org

Pennsylvania: CHAPKimH@aol.com

Rhode Island: right_right@mailexcite.com

South Carolina: schea1@aol.com

Tennessee: jcthornton3@earthlink.net

Texas: staff@thsc.org

Utah: utch@utch.org

Virginia: vhea@juno.com

Washington: Rlisk@aol.com

West Virginia: chewvadm@aol.com

Wisconsin: jang@execpc.com

Wyoming: mungermtrr@compuserve.com

State Homeschooling Organizations

When researching your state's homeschooling laws and regulations, we recommend you contact the HSLDA Web site first at http://www.hslda.org, then the parent-run state organization, second, and the state department of education last.

Alabama

Home Educators of Alabama Roundtable (HEART),
    (256) 890-0515, http://www.heartofalabama

Alabama State Department of Education, (334) 242-8165

Alaska

Alaska Private & Home Educators Association (APHEA),
    (907) 566-3450, http://www.aphea.org

Alaska Department of Education, (907) 465-2800

Arizona

Arizona Families for Home Education (AFHE), 1-800-929-3927
In Maricopa County, (602) 443-0612,
http://www.primenet.com/~afhe

Arizona Department of Education, (602) 542-4361

Arkansas

Home Educators of Arkansas, (501) 847-4942

Arkansas Homeschooling Resource Directory (AHRD),
2703 Grist Mill Rd., Little Rock, AR 72227

Arkansas Department of Education, (501) 682-4251

California

California Homeschool Network (CHN), 1-800-327-5339,
http://www.cahomeschoolnet.org

Homeschool Association of California (HSC), 1-888-HSC-4440,
http://www.hsc.org

California Department of Education, (916) 657-2453

Colorado

Christian Home Educators of Colorado (CHEC), (303) 338-1888,
http://www.chec.org

Colorado Home Educators Association, (303) 441-9938

Colorado State Board of Education, (303) 866-6817

Connecticut

Connecticut Home Educators Association (CHEA),
(203) 781-8569, http://www.connix.com/~dschroth/chea/
RCT.html

The Education Association of Christian Homeschoolers (TEACH),
within Connecticut 1-800-205-7844, outside Connecticut
(860) 231-2930

Connecticut Department of Education, (860) 566-8263 or
(860) 566-5982

Delaware

Delaware Home Education Association (DHEA), (302) 475-0574

Delaware Department of Education, (302) 739-4583

Florida

Florida Parent Educator's Association, 1-877-275-3732

Florida Department of Education, (850) 487-8428

Georgia

Georgia Home Education Association (GHEA), (770) 461-3657,
http://www.ghea.org

Georgia Department of Education, (404) 656-2446

Hawaii

The Hawaii Homeschool Association, (808) 944-3339

Hawaii Department of Education, (808) 733-9895

Idaho

Idaho Coalition of Home Educators, (208) 264-5212

Idaho Department of Education, (208) 332-6800

Illinois

Home Oriented Unique Schooling Experience (HOUSE),
(708) 758-7374, http://www.geocities.com/Athens/
Acropolis/7804

Illinois Christian Home Educators, (847) 662-1909

Illinois State Board of Education, (217) 782-3950

Indiana

Indiana Association of Home Educators (Christian),
    (317) 859-1202

Indiana Department of Education, (317) 232-9135

Iowa

Iowa Department of Education, (515) 281-5294

Kansas

Christian Home Educators Conference of Kansas (CHECK),
    (785) 843-9207, http://www.kansashomeschool.org

Teaching Parents Association (TPA), (316) 945-0810

Kansas State Department of Education, (785) 296-3201

Kentucky

Christian Home Educators of Kentucky (CHEK), (502) 358-9270,
    http://www.chek.org

Kentucky Home Education Association (KHEA), (606) 737-3338,
    http://www.ky-on-line.com/bhe

Kentucky Department of Education, (502) 564-3791

Louisiana

Christian Home Educators Fellowship of Louisiana,
    1-888-876-2433

Louisiana Home Education Network (LAHEN),
    http://www.members.aol.com/La-HomeED/Lahen.html

Louisiana Department of Education, (504) 342-3473

Maine

Maine Home Education Associates, 1-800-520-0577

Maine Department of Education, (207) 287-5922

Maryland

Maryland Home Education Association, (410) 730-0073

Maryland State Department of Education, (410) 767-0288

Massachusetts

The Massachusetts Home Learning Association, (508) 429-1436

Mass H.O.P.E., (508) 755-4467

Massachusetts Department of Education, (781) 388-3300

Michigan

The Homeschool Support Network (HSN), (734) 284-1249

Michigan Department of Education, (517) 335-4074

Minnesota

Homebased Educators' Accrediting Association, (651) 223-0333

Minnesota Homeschoolers Alliance, (612) 288-9662

Minnesota Department of Children, Families, & Learning,
    (651) 582-8593

Mississippi

Mississippi Home Educators Association (MHEA),
    (601) 833-9110

Mississippi Department of Education, (601) 359-2098

Missouri

Families for Home Education (FHE), (417) 782-8833

Missouri Department of Education, (573) 751-3527

Montana

Montana Coalition of Home Educators, (406) 587-6163,
    http://www.3.gomontana.com/white/mche.html

Montana Department of Education, (406) 444-3095

Nebraska

Nebraska Christian Home Education Association (NCHEA),
(402) 423-4297

Nebraska Department of Education, (402) 471-2784

Nevada

Home Schools United Vegas Valley, (702) 870-9566

Nevada Department of Education, (775) 687-9134

New Hampshire

New Hampshire Homeschool Coalition, (603) 539-7233

New Hampshire Department of Education, (603) 271-3144

New Jersey

North Jersey Home Schoolers Association (NJHSA),
(201) 666-6025

Educational Network of Christian Homeschoolers (ENOCH),
(732) 291-7800

New Jersey Department of Education, (609) 984-7814

New Mexico

New Mexico Family Educators, (505) 275-7053

New Mexico Department of Education, (505) 827-6582

New York

Loving Education at Home (LEAH), (716) 346-0939,
http://www.leah.org

New York Home Education Network (NYHEN), (518) 584-9110

Alliance for Parental Involvement in Education (ALLPIE),
(518) 392-6900, http://www.croton.com/allpie

Office for Nonpublic School Services, (518) 474-3879

North Carolina

North Carolinians for Home Education, (919) 834-6243

Division of Nonpublic Education, (919) 733-4276

North Dakota

North Dakota Homeschool Association, (701) 223-4080

North Dakota Department of Public Instruction, (701) 328-4572

Ohio

Ohio Home Educators Network (OHEN), (330) 274-0542

Ohio Department of Education, (614) 466-2937

Oklahoma

Home Educator's Resource Organization (HERO) of Oklahoma,
(918) 396-0108, http://www.geocities.com/Athens/Forum/
3236

Oregon

Oregon Home Education Network (OHEN), (503) 321-5166

Oregon Christian Home Education Network (OCEAN),
(503) 288-1285

Parents Political Action Committee (PPAC), (503) 693-0724

Oregon Department of Education, (503) 378-5585, ext. 677

Pennsylvania

Pennsylvania Home Education Network, (412) 561-5288

Catholic Homeschoolers of Pennsylvania, (717) 866-5425

School Services Unit of the Pennsylvania Department of
    Education, (717) 787-4860

Rhode Island

Rhode Island Guild of Home Teachers (RIGHT), (401) 821-7700

Rhode Island Department of Education, (401) 222-4600, ext. 2503

South Carolina

South Carolina Association of Independent Homeschools (SCAIHS),
    (803) 551-1003, http://www.scaihs.org

South Carolina Home Educators Association (SCHEA),
    (803) 754-6425, http://members.aol.com/schea1/index.
    html

South Carolina Department of Education, (803) 734-8493

South Dakota

Western Dakota Christian Home Schools (Support Group),
    (605) 745-4203

South Dakota Department of Education, (605) 773-6934

Tennessee

Tennessee Home Education Association, (615) 834-3529,
    http://www.MemphisHomeEd.org

Tennessee Department of Education, (615) 741-2731

Texas

Texas Homeschool Coalition (THC), (806) 797-4927,
    http://www.thsc.org

Texas Education Agency, (512) 463-9734

Utah

Utah Home Education Association (UHEA), 1-888-887-UHEA, http://www.itsnet.com/~uhea

Utah State Office of Education, (801) 538-7801

Vermont

Vermont Homeschoolers Directory, (802) 259-3493

Vermont Department of Education, (802) 828-5406

Virginia

Virginia Home Education Association (VHEA), (540) 832-3578

Virginia Department of Education, (804) 786-9421

Washington

The Washington Homeschool Organization, (425) 251-0439

Family Learning Organization, (509) 467-2552

Washington State Board of Education, (360) 753-6715

West Virginia

West Virginia Department of Education, http://www.wvde.state.wv.us

Wisconsin

Wisconsin Parents Association (WPA), (608) 283-3131

Wisconsin Department of Public Instruction, (608) 266-3390

Wyoming

Homeschoolers of Wyoming, (307) 733-2834

Wyoming Department of Education, (307) 777-7670

Web Sites for Homeschoolers

Activities for Learning, e-mail: joancott@hutchtel.net

Alpha-Phonics, http://www.alpha-phonics.com

Atco School Supply, Inc., http://www.atco1.com

The Back Pack, http://www.thebackpack.com

The Book Cellar, e-mail: bookcellar@juno.com

The Book Peddler, e-mail: TheBookPeddler@juno.com

Bridgestone OnLine Academy, http://www. switched-on
schoolhouse.com/bola

Chalk Dust Company, http://www.chalkdust.com

Christian Liberty Academy, http://www.homeschools.org

Eagle Christian School, http://www.eaglechristian. org

Edusoft, http://www.edusoftonline.com

Excellence in Writing, http://www.writing-edu.com

The Helping Hand, http://rampages.onramp.net/~classics

Life Pathways, http://www.findafuture.com

Math Concepts, Inc., http://www.mathconcepts.com

Math-U-See, http://www.mathusee.com

Natural Speller, http://www.designastudy.com

Power-Glide, http://www.power-glide.com

Pulliam Journalism Fellowships, http://www.starnews.com/pif

Runkle Geography, e-mail: info@runklepub.com

Saxon Publishers, Inc., http://www.saxonpub.com

School of Tomorrow, http://www.schooloftomorrow.com

StartWrite, http://www.startwrite.com

The Teaching Home, http://www.TeachingHome.com

Writing Strands, http://www.writingstrands.com

APPENDIX A

Official Transcript Sample

Place signature or seal here

ACADEMIC ACHIEVEMENT RECORD

Principal/Teacher: _____

Student: _____ Date of Birth: _____

Address: _____

Student's Social Security Number: _____

School Year	Subject	Final Grades Semester 1	Final Grades Semester 2	Credits Earned
Grade 9	English I	97	98	1
	Algebra I	93	94	1
	Gen. Science	89	89	1
	U.S. History	90	91	1
	Spanish I	81	83	1
	Keyboarding	100	—	½
	Music/Piano	100	100	1
	P.E./CHSA	100	100	1
	Health	—	98	½
Total Credits Earned				**8**
Grade Point Average				**3.75**

School Year	Subject	Final Grades Semester 1	Semester 2	Credits Earned
Grade 10	English II	96	97	1
	Geometry	98	99	1
	Biology	88	91	1
	World History	94	94	1
	Spanish II	80	87	1
	Computer Sci.	100	—	½
	Music/Flute	100	100	1
	P.E./Karate	100	100	1
	Driver's Ed.	—	96	½
Total Credits Earned				**16**
Grade Point Average				**3.78**
Grade 11	English III	96	99	1
	Algebra II	94	93	1
	Chemistry	87	90	1
	Spanish III	88	85	1
	Computer Sci.	—	100	½
	Weight Training	100	100	1
	Work	—	100	½
Total Credits Earned				**22**
Grade Point Average				**3.68**
Grade 12	English IV	97	97	1
	Government	88	90	1
	Speech	—	95	½
	Marketing	95	—	½
	Weight Training	100	100	1
	Work	100	100	1
Total Credits Earned				**27**
Grade Point Average				**3.50**
College courses	English 101	99	99	3
(taken in senior	Psychology A-101	100	99	3
year)	Geology 2294	97	100	3

EXTRACURRICULAR ACTIVITIES

CHSA Homeschool Basketball	4 years
Meadows Swim All Stars	4 years
Volunteer Read to a Child Program	2 years
Volunteer Read to Me Program	2 years
Published Children's Story/*Highlights*	see attachment
Pencil Drawing Award/*Art World Magazine*	see attachment

SCHOLARSHIPS AWARDED

CHSA Athletic Scholarship	$2,500
Academic Merit Award Musclemania	$4,000

Sample Four-Year Plan of Study for Graduation

Name: _____ **Date Started:** _____

Indicate regular, vocational, or advanced course as R, V, or A.

Subject	Semester 1	Semester 2	Course (R,V,A)

Sample Elementary, Middle, or High School Report Card

Grade Level: _____ **School Year:** _____

Student: _____

Address: _____

Course	Semester 1	Semester 2	Year-End Grade

Awards	Activities

Reading List (title, author)

_____

_____

_____

_____

_____

_____

_____

_____

_____

BIBLIOGRAPHY

Brandt, Sue R. *Facts About the 50 States.* Franklin Watts, 1979.

Colvin, Ruth J., and Jane H. Root, Ph.D. *Tutor Techniques Used in the Teaching of Reading.* Literacy Volunteers of America, 1987.

Davis, Susan, H. "Baseball and Study Skills." *Homeschooling Today* 8, no. 2 (March/April 1999): 17–18.

Editors of the Teaching Home. "Home-School Organizations." *The Teaching Home* 17, no. 1 (January/February 1999): 31–33.

Farris, Michael. "Legal News." *The Teaching Home* 17, no. 1, (January/February 1999): 29–30

Gerald, Debra E., and William J. Husser. National Center for Education Statistics.

Gordon, George Noel, Lord Byron, and Betty Burger. "The Destruction of Sennacherib. Living Literature for Middle Grades." *Homeschooling Today* 8, no. 2 (March/April 1999): 21.

HOPE for Texas. *Handbook for Texas Home Schoolers.* Dallas: HOPE for Texas, 1995.

The New York Public Library Student's Desk Reference. New York: Stonesong Press, 1993.

Parker, Debbie L. "College Success: Views of Home School Graduates." *Home School Helper* 11, no. 2 (April 1999): 1–3.

Projections of Education Statistics to 2005. U.S. Dept. of Education, Jan. 1995.

Robinson, Adam, and John Katzman. *The Princeton Review Cracking the SAT & PSAT, 1996 Edition.* New York: Random House, 1995.

Web Sites

http://info.rutgers.edu/Library/Reference/US/constitution/9

http://www.house.gov

http://www.senate.gov

INDEX